THE HUNCHBACK

Borgo Press Books Translated by FRANK J. MORLOCK

The Boss Lady: A Play in Five Acts by Paul Féval
The Hunchback: A Play in Five Acts, by Auguste Anicet-Bourgeois and Paul Féval

THE HUNCHBACK

A PLAY IN FIVE ACTS

AUGUSTE ANICET-

BOURGEOIS & PAUL FÉVAL

Translated and Adapted by Frank J. Morlock

THE BORGO PRESS
MMXI

THE HUNCHBACK

Copyright © 2004, 2011 by Frank J. Morlock

FIRST EDITION

Published by Wildside Press LLC

www.wildsidebooks.com

DEDICATION

For my new friend,

Ben Meade

CONTENTS

CAST OF CHARACTERS	9
PROLOGUE, Scene 1	11
PROLOGUE, Scene 2	31
ACT I, Scene 3	43
ACT I, Scene 4	68
ACT II, Scene 5	74
ACT II, Scene 6	93
ACT III, Scene 7	106
ACT III, Scene 8	118
ACT IV, Scene 9	138
ACT IV, Scene 10	146
ACT V, Scene 11	169
ABOUT THE AUTHOR	175

CAST OF CHARACTERS

LAGARDÈRE
GONZAGUE
CHAVERNY
THE REGENT
NEVERS
NAVAILLE
COCARDASSE
PASSEPOIL
D'ARGENSON
BONNIVET
TONIO
PEYROLLES
CARRIGUE
STAUPITZ
NATHANIEL
BREANT
LACROIX
FIRST BOURGEOIS
SECOND BOURGEOIS
AN ARCHITECT
BLANCHE DE CAYLUS
BLANCHE DE NEVERS
FLORA
PEPITA
A PAGE
ANGÉLIQUE

MADELEINE
MARTON

PROLOGUE
SCENE 1

The Adam's Apple Inn. A room in a hotel on the frontier of France and Spain. To the right, near the audience, a window opening on the moats of the Château. Further back, in cutaway, a gate opening on the street. To the left, near the audience, a door opening on a garden. To the left, at the back, an entry with two doors, between them a tall dresser, Tables, chairs, etc, etc.

Martine is hurriedly arranging bowls and glasses. Peyrolles is by the door at the left.

MARTINE: With what sort of characters have you arranged a meeting at my place?

PEYROLLES: (pointing to six rapiers hanging on the wall.) Swordsmen.

MARTINE: Rather of sack and rope.

PEYROLLES: No news yet of the little page of Mr. de Nevers?

MARTINE: Of that poor lad you made me put to sleep by means of I don't know what drug mixed in his wine?

PEYROLLES: He hasn't returned with a reply to the letter?

MARTINE: The one you took from him in his sleep?

PEYROLLES: Oh, just borrowed, merely borrowed, dame Martine. I faithfully put it back in his pocket.

MARTINE: Yes, after having read it, and copied it even.

PEYROLLES: Did he notice?

MARTINE: Aren't you a sorcerer, Mr. Peyrolles?

PEYROLLES: I'm not clumsy, that's all. (going to the door at the right) Where are my braves?

MARTINE: Your strong breed? They were under the tunnel gambling when they are not drinking, drinking when they are not gambling.

PEYROLLES: I am expecting two others, the best, Master Cocardesse the younger, and Amable Passepoil, his provost.

MARTINE: Again!

VOICE (from the tunnel) Wine! Wine! (Martine goes into the room at the right)

PEYROLLES: Give these gentlemen all that they ask for.

MARTINE: Nice work! Happily, you're the one who's paying! Were it not for that—

VOICES: Wine! Wine!

PEYROLLES: I will return once they're full. Let them drink but keep them quiet.

(Peyrolles leaves)

MARTINE: I will never be able to prevent those demons from continuing their Sabbath. What's that I hear on the highway? Is it at least a practicing Christian who's coming to me?

(looking) Ah! Those are the two bandits that Mr. de Peyrolles is expecting. They are more sinister than the others.

COCARDASSE: (appearing) Hey! Goddam! Here it's been two hours that we've seen this devil of a château on its mountain; it seems to me it moves as fast as we do. Finally, we've got it. (enters and swaggers with an impudent pride) Have no fear, my snail, come in, my good man, we are in port.

PASSEPOIL: Throw us an anchor.

COCARDASSE: Sonofabitch! Wine! (taking the bowl on the table and drinking)

PASSEPOIL: (noticing Martine) Son of a bitch! A woman! (grabbing her by the waist and trying to kiss her)

MARTINE: (escaping) Help! Help!

PASSEPOIL: Let's not shout, Venus. Come on, a little kiss, Queen of Love.

MARTINE: That fat guy is crazy!

PASSEPOIL: I am mad, yes, but I am not fat. It seems I have a heart that's not common. It keeps getting bigger, and, as the body envelops the heart, naturally, the body enlarges. But I am all heart, beauty of beauties, and this heart is yours!

MARTINE: Let me go or I scream fire!

COCARDASSE: (who's been drinking) Caramba! Can't you even control your passions?

PASSEPOIL: I'm only asking for a kiss on the hand.

MARTINE: My hand! Here it is. (smacking him and moving away)

PASSEPOIL: It's still a favor. From a woman all is good.

MARTINE: Then let me go announce you to the others.

COCARDASSE: They've got here. Er, yes, dammit! I see their rapiers. Announce to them, Cocardasse, Jr.

PASSEPOIL: And Amable Passepoil, who is addressing you, Calypso.

COCARDASSE: They've seen us. They're rushing to meet us, here they are.

ALL: Cocardasse!

PASSEPOIL: (aside) Oh, villainous faces!

COCARDASSE: Have no fear! All friends. (they exchange hand grips)

STAUPITZ: (at the table) Wine, as if it were raining, to celebrate the arrival of friends.

MARTINE: (serving) Here, here. You need a flood to satisfy you.

PASSEPOIL: A flood of kisses, my beautiful angel!

MARTINE: I debit only whacks.

COCARDASSE: By Jove! We are here to speak seriously; be gone, little one, you are inflaming him.

MARTINE: Get out? I ask nothing better. (she leaves)

COCARDASSE: Women will be the ruin of this little fellow. Now, my pretties, let's talk about our business. There are eight of us here. All professors of the art of swordsmanship! Each of us can hold his head against three men properly handling the sword: In that case, are we going to have a dust-up with an army?

STAUPITZ: No, we are going to have business with a single cavalier.

COCARDASSE: And what then is the name of this giant who fights against eight men worth half a dozen heroes by Jove!

STAUPITZ: It's Duke Philippe de Nevers.

CARCADASSE: (grimacing) Him! Him!

PASSEPOIL: (imitating him) Him! Him!

ALL: What's wrong with you?

STAUPITZ: It seems you want to abandon the party?

PASSEPOIL: We saw the Duke de Nevers in Paris. He's a chap that will settle your accounts.

ALL: (shouting) Ours!

COCARDASSE: You've never heard tell of the thrust of

Nevers?

STAUPITZ: Just balderdash these secret thrusts!

ALL: Yes, yes.

COCARDASSE: (proudly) Sonofabitch! I think I've got a good foot, and good eye, and good guard, my pretties, and yet I was touched three times in a row right in front of my whole academy.

PASSEPOIL: In our own academy!

COCARDASSE: There's one man alone capable of holding his head with Philippe de Nevers, sword in hand.

PASSEPOIL: One alone.

ALL: And this man?

COCARDASSE: It's a little Parisian, the Chevalier Henri de Lagardère.

(A moment of silence, the bravos look at each other)

STAUPITZ: The one who killed all the Flemish provosts beneath the walls of Senlis?

COCARDASSE: There's only one Lagardère, Here's Mr. de Peyrolles, the agent of the Prince of Gonzague! Gentlemen, the thrust of Nevers is worth gold, let my noble friend and myself act, and whatever we say to this Peyrolles, support us. And those who tonight, have not had their thighs pierced by the sword of Philippe de Nevers will have enough money to empty a cask to the memory of the deceased.

(Peyrolles enters. All rise and bow to him)

PEYROLLES: (after having counted with his eyes) Here you all are, my masters, that's fine. Shut that door. I am going to tell you briefly what you will have to do.

COCARDASSE: (to the table) We are listening, my good Mr. de Peyrolles. (leaning on his elbows) Well then?

PEYROLLES: (at the window) This evening, around nine o'clock, a man will come on this highway you see here. Look, there in the ditches beneath the drawbridge, all is rising; do you notice a low window closed by oak shutters?

COCARDASSE: Perfectly, my good Mr. Peyrolles.

PASSEPOIL: Perfectly, my good Mr. Peyrolles.

ALL: Perfectly.

PEYROLLES: The man will approach this window.

COCARDASSE: And, at that moment we will accost him.

PEYROLLES: (laughing) Politely.

ALL: Politely.

PEYROLLES: And you will earn all your money.

COCARDASSE: This good Mr. Peyrolles; there's still a word to be said.

PEYROLLES: It's agreed.

ALL: Agreed.

(Peyrolles makes a move to leave.)

COCARDASSE: How can you speak like this without revealing to us the name of the man we are to accost—politely?

PEYROLLES: What's it to you?

COCARDASSE: (coming forward) Dear me! You didn't tell me that this nocturnal visitor is none other than the Prince Philippe de Lorraine, Duke of Nevers, who is the best blade in France and Navarre.

PEYROLLES: There will be eight of you against him.

COCARDASSE: To begin with, but who knows if even one will remain at the end?

PEYROLLES: Come on!

COCARDASSE Hum! From the moment it's a question of Mr. de Nevers—

PEYROLLES: You hesitate?

COCARDASSE: No, I refuse. I don't know if my little provost Passepoil will be more enterprising than I am.

PASSEPOIL: I'm leaving.

PEYROLLES: You want to laugh my funny fellows! If the job is more difficult, we will pay more dearly, that's all.

COCARDASSE: With men of wit one always comes to an agreement.

PASSEPOIL: One always comes to an agreement.

COCARDASSE: What sum was agreed on?

STAUPITZ: Two hundred miserly pistoles!

CAOCARDASSE: I want, hum, two thousand, two thousand. Is that enough, my pebble?

PASSEPOIL: No.

COCARDASSE: The little fellow says no.

PEYROLLES: Cut short the verbiage. What do you want?

COCARDASSE: Three thousand pistoles.

PEYROLLES: Agreed.

COCARDASSE: Is that enough, my pebble?

PASSEPOIL: Yes.

COCARDASSE: The little fellow says yes.

PEYROLLLES: That's lucky.

COCARDASSE: Deal done.

PEYROLLES: Shake.

(Cocardasse looks at his hand without taking it; then he raps his hand on his sword, gesture by Peyrolles)

COCARDASSE: There's the scrivener who answers to me for you, my good man.

(he bows affectedly, all imitate him)

PEYROLLES: (ready to leave) If you fail, you get nothing

COCARDASSE: That goes without saying.

(Peyrolles leaves, everyone bursts out laughing)

COCARDASSE: Wine! Something to drink!

(Staupitz, Pinto, and Faenza have accompanied Peyrolles to the door, making an ironic bow)

SHOUTS (outside) Help! Help!

COCARDASSE: What's that?

STAUPITZ: Those are partisans coming to forage in the moats of the Castle.

COCARDASSE: Those clowns are bold. How many are they?

STAUPITZ: (at the door, counting) Three, Four, Six, Eight.

COCARDASSE: Exactly as many as us. We could laugh a bit.

PASSEPOIL: Exactly. I'm beginning to get bored. There they are.

CARRIGUE: This way, gentlemen.

COCARDASSE: My masters, I think it's time to unhook your rapiers. (they gird on their swords) Now we will be in ranks. (they go back to the table, all elbows are touching)

CARRIGUE (outside) There's one thing.

CORCADASSE: We say the best way to keep on guard is a left

handed provost.

CARRIGUE: (in the doorway) Holá! The inn is full. It must be emptied. (they enter) There, beat it, and fast; there's only room here for volunteers of the king. (all the bravos want to leave; Cocardasse stops them)

COCARDASSE: Stay put. Let's be sociable and make these gentleman volunteers of the king dance in tune. (they rise and bow with excessive politeness)

CARRIGUE: Can't you see we need your tables and your stools!

COCARDASSE: Have no fear. We're going to give you all that, my pretties.

(taking a jug and breaking it over Carrigue's head) These gentlemen are served.

CARRIGUE & HIS MEN: Forward! Lagardère! Lagardère!

(Cocardasse and Passepoil let their swords fall)

COCARDASSE Down with your weapons everybody!

PASSEPOIL: What was it you said?

COCARDASSE: Whose name did you utter?

STAUPITZ: We were going to gobble them up like sparrows.

COCARDASSE: Peace! Why did you shout Lagardère?

CARRIGUE: Because Lagardère is our captain.

COCARDASSE: The Chevalier Henri de Lagardère?

CARRIGUE: Yes.

COCARDASSE: Our Parisian?

PASSEPOIL: Our jewel?

COCARDASSE: One moment; no confusion. We left Lagardère in Paris, Light Cavalry-Man of the King.

CARRIGUE: Yes, but he was bored being a light cavalry man. All he's kept is the uniform and he commands a company of royal volunteers here in the valley.

COCARDESSE: Then stop, swords in scabbards. Long live God! Friends of the Parisian and ours, and we are all going to drink together to the first blade in the universe! To table!

ALL: To table!

COCARDASSE: Hey! I don't feel any joy! Wine. (to Passepoil) Hang on! (to Carrigue) I have the honor of presenting to you my apprentice, Passepoil, who—be it said without offending you, is going to demonstrate to you a maneuver of which you haven't the least notion. (Passepoil bows)

PASSEPOIL: My noble friend, Cocardasse Junior, the most humble admirer, after myself of Mr. de Lagardère.

COCARDASSE: And I boast of it, sonofabitch! It's I who gave him his first lesson in arms. Ah! He gave me promise, but Jove, how he turned out!

A CHEVALIER: (to Carrigue) Hey, Commandant, look down there!

CARRIGUE: By God, it's that little wise guy who got our horses breathless in his pursuit. He's going to pass under this window. Grab him and bring him here. (Two men leave) This domain of Caylus is near Rambouillet where Mr. d'Orléans often hunts. And this little fellow could be a poacher.

(The Page is brought in by two cavaliers)

CARRIGUE: Come here, little wise guy.

COCARDASSE : Have no fear. We won't skin you alive.

PASSEPOIL: He's nice this little fellow. He belongs to some lady. Let's see, little one, to whom are you taking a love letter?

PAGE: Me? I'm not taking anything.

PASSEPOIL: Who do you serve?

PAGE: I don't serve anyone.

COCARDASSE: Damn it! Do you think we have time to play at guessing games? Come on, by Jove, let him be searched.

PAGE: (pulling a dagger) Don't touch me!

COCARDASSE: Ah, you bite, little wolf-cub! (They surround the page, knock him down and begin searching him. Lagardère appears, violently pushes Cocardasse to one side and on the other Passepoil who rolls onto his companions.)

COCARDASSE: Sonofabitch!

PASSEPOIL: Cunt! (recognizing Lagardère) Heaven!

COCARDASSE: Great God!

PASSEPOIL: The Parisian!

COCARDASSE: Lagardère!

ALL: (bowing with respect) Captain Lagardère—

LAGARDÈRE: What the devil are you doing so far from the street of Croix des Petits Champs, my two masters?

COCARDASSE: Formerly, but today your servants, O great man.

PASSEPOIL: Your slaves.

LAGARDÈRE And this one? (pointing to Staupitz) I've seen him somewhere!

STAUPITZ: At Strasbourg, Captain (rubbing his shoulder) I recall it.

LAGARDÈRE: Staupitz, isn't it? Ah, ah! Jouel! Saldagne, Pinto. We met at Bayenne, I think? And Matador Faenza—I recognize you all and you all bear my marks. (to Page) Come here, child, tell me what you are doing in this inn?

PAGE: I'm coming to bring a letter, Captain.

LAGARDÈRE: To whom?

PAGE: To you.

LAGARDÈRE: To me? Give it to me.

PAGE: (low) I had another one for a lady and I really wanted—

LAGARDÈRE: (tossing him his purse) Go, little one. No one will disturb you. My volunteers will escort you.

PAGE: Thanks, Captain (leaves with others)

LAGARDÈRE: (opening the letter as everyone comes close to him) Make room. I prefer to open my correspondence alone. (the others move away, hats down) By Heaven! He's a true gentleman, this Nevers.

ALL: Nevers!

LAGARDÈRE: (seated in Cocardasse's place) Something to drink, first of all. My heart is content. I have to tell you I am exiled.

COCARDASSE: Exiled!

PASSEPOIL: You!

LAGARDÈRE: Eh, my God, yes! Do you know that huge devil of a Belissen?

COCARDASSE: Baron Belissen?

PASSEPOIL: Belissen the Duelist?

LAGARDÈRE: The deceased Belissen.

COCARDASSE: He's dead?

LAGARDÈRE: Naturally, since I killed him. He wanted to play insults with me, and that displeased me, and as I promised His Majesty when he deigned to create me a knight, not to cast injurious words at anyone, I pulled his ears. That was not to his taste.

COCARDASSE: I believe it.

LAGARDÈRE: He said so to me very loudly—and behind the Arsenal I gave him a straight goodbye blow—to the depths.

COCARDASSE: (forgetting himself) Ah, rogue! How well you stretched him out. That blow—

LAGARDÈRE: (rising) To whom are you speaking?

COCARDASSE: (bowing) Ah, pardon, pardon!

LAGARDÈRE: There's justice. They owe me the best since I beat a wolf-head! They exiled me, but I swore that I won't cross the frontier without allowing myself a last fantasy. (he raps on the letter) Tell me, my valiants, you've heard tell of the thrust of Nevers?

ALL: By Jove!

LAGARDÈRE: This cursed thrust was my *bête-noir*; it prevented me from sleeping, besides this Nevers talked too much of it at court, in town, in the cabaret, in quarters. I heard only one name, Nevers, Nevers. One night, my hostess was serving me cutlets *à la* Nevers. I threw the dish out the window and left without supper. At the gate, I yelled at my shoe-maker who was bringing me boots—*à la* Nevers, the latest fashion! I beat up my bootmaker and threw ten crowns in his face. The wise guy said to me, "Ah, Mr. de Nevers beat me once, but he gave me a hundred pistoles."

CORCADASSE: That's too much.

LAGARDÈRE: I jumped on my horse and went to await Nevers at the exit from the Louvre. "Duke," I said to him, "I have great confidence in your courtesy; I am coming to ask you to show me your secret thrust in the moonlight" He looked at me and said, "Your name?" "Lagardère." "Ah, ah, you are Lagardère. They often mention you to me and that bores me. So, if you don't find me much, little gentleman," he jumped on his horse, Ah, I have to say he did it charmingly: instead of replying to me he placed his rapier between my two eyebrows, so roughly and so fast but for a leap of two bounds that I made backwards. "Again, a short lesson, Duke." "At your service, Chevalier." I told you he was charming. "We will fall back on guard—plague!" This time he gave me a scratch on the face. I was troubled, me, Lagardère.

(All the Bravos look at Lagardère and move past him.)

COCARDASSE: *Caramba!* That's scary!

LAGARDÈRE: I hadn't reached the parade yet. That man's as quick as powder. But I had seen the feint, Goddam! I had studied him in the silence of the closet, and now I possess him as well as you!

COCARDASSE: It could serve you one day.

LAGARDÈRE: It will serve me right away.

COCARDASSE: What do you mean?

LAGARDÈRE: Nevers has promised me revenge. I wrote him at his Château, and his response is: he accepts the meeting, the hour and the place.

COCARDASSE: What day?

LAGARDÈRE: Tonight.

PASSEPOIL: The time?

LAGARDÈRE: Nine o'clock.

COCARDASSE: The place?

LAGARDÈRE: The moats of the Château of Caylus!

COCARDASSE: (looking at the bravos) Sonofabitch! And why this place?

LAGARDÈRE: Second fantasy, I allowed myself to say that the old Marquis de Caylus had the most beautiful daughter in the world and that Mr. de Nevers was in love with her. Well, I want to take from Mr. de Nevers his mysterious thrust and his mysterious mistress. Why aren't you laughing, my wise guys?

COCARDASSE: Is it that in your letter to Mr. de Nevers you had the trashy idea of mentioning Miss Blanche de Caylus to him?

PASSEPOIL: We are thinking, Chevalier, that it is really fortunate that we will be here to serve you.

COCARDASSE: The kid's right; we are going to give you a famous hand. Isn't that right, the rest of you?

LAGARDÈRE: And since when have I lost the habit of managing my own affairs myself? On my soul, here are some pleasant buffoons with their service. One final drink and empty the place for me—now that's the only service I can ask of you.

COCARDASSE: Dammit! Captain, I'd get myself killed like a dog for you, but—

LAGARDÈRE: But what—?

COCARDASSE: Each of us has his profession you know. And we cannot leave this place.

LAGARDÈRE: Because?

COCARDASSE: Because we are also waiting for someone.

LAGARDÈRE: And this someone is?

COCARDASSE: This someone is—Philippe de Nevers.

LAGARDÈRE: Nevers? You? A trap?

PASSEPOIL: But—

LAGARDÈRE: Peace, my wise guys! I forbid you—you understand me plainly enough—I forbid you to touch a hair on Nevers—because his life belongs to me, and if he must die it will be by my hand in honest battle, not by yours, bandits!

COCARDASSE: Captain!

LAGARDÈRE: Go!

PASSEPOIL: After all, if he wants to do our work—

COCARDASSE: (low) Very well. But we must keep an eye on Nevers. If this little Parisian fails, we won't.

LAGARDÈRE: You understand me.

COCARDASSE: Yes, Captain.

LAGARDÈRE: No treachery! No ambush! Who's against Nevers is against me. Be gone, wise guys, and don't let one of you show himself here in the future, because I won't honor that one with a sword blow—in place of my sword, I will whip his hang-dog face.

COCARDASSE: Sonofabitch, Captain! You are forgetting that we are soldiers.

LAGARDÈRE: You! Get out! Whoever kills for money is infamous, whoever uses a dagger rather than a rapier is a coward. Soldiers and braves, that's what you were, and I knew you then, infamous and cowards, that's what you are. I no longer know you. Leave!

(At Lagardère's gesture, all bow and leave.)

PASSEPOIL: He's very harsh.

COCARDASSE: (low) As for him, we will always know him.

(He leaves with Passepoil)

LAGARDÈRE: The wretches! Eight against one! Oh, that's disgusting to the sword! Girl! (the hostess appears, Lagardère tosses a gold coin on the table) Close the shutters and put up the bars. Whatever you may hear in the moats of the castle tonight, you and your folks, sleep on both ears; they are affairs that do not concern you. Goodbye.

(he leaves)

CURTAIN

PROLOGUE
SCENE 2

The moats of the castle connected by a ditch on the right and by a bridge that faces the audience and reaches the tower of the château from which a balcony projects underneath which is a small window; it's there that stacks of hay are heaped up; a loaded cart is on the side. To the left, a stairway, at the back a large opening.

LAGARDÈRE: (getting his bearings before going into the moat) Ah, let's try not to break our neck. (going down the stairway) It's as dark as in an oven; we must fence carefully. It will be delightful. (testing the ground with his foot) What's that? Grass. No solid ground. Perfect. Now, let's orient ourselves. (groping at the low window) A window! Bravo! For a love adventure after a sword adventure here's our entrance. Ah! the devil of a shutter. Someone's coming down. I hear walking. Will it be Nevers already? He's going to arrive very angry, this dear Duke. We have only to be quite ready.

(Gonzague and Peyrolles arrive wrapped in cloaks at the head of the bridge, and attempt to see into the distance.)

GONZAGUE: I don't see anyone.

PEYROLLES: Indeed, Down there—near the window.

GONZAGUE: (stopping) Suppose he's not one of us?

PEYROLLES: Impossible! I directed a sentinel be left here. It's Staupitz. I recognize him. Staupitz.

LAGARDÈRE: Present.

PEYROLLES: (to Gonzague) You see! You can go down, Duke.

LAGAREDERRE: Ah, he's a Duke!

GONZAGUE: To the devil with your manners! You might as well tell them my name.

LAGARDÈREE: I would really like to know it.

GONZAGUE: Will Philippe come?

PEYROLLES: Don't you recall the very urgent letter sent him by Miss Blanche de Caylus? He will come to deliver himself into our hands; once we kill the father, we will seize the child.

LAGARDÈRE: They are lowering their voices. I cannot hear a thing.

GONZAGUE: No, it's better to begin by capturing and making this child of Nevers vanish; the hour approaches. What sort of man is this Staupitz?

PEYROLLES: A determined rogue.

GONZAGUE: That can be relied on?

PEYROLLES: If well paid, yes.

GONZAGUE: Call him!

LAGARDÈRE: (aside) Could this be the leader of the assassins?

PEYROLLES: Staupitz!

LAGARDÈRE: Present!

PEYROLLES: Advance!

GONZAGUE: Would you like to earn fifty pistoles?

LAFARDERRE: What has to be done?

GONZAGUE: Stay at your post under this window and wait until nine o'clock strikes. Then you will rap at the shutter of this window which will open and you will say two words to the woman who opens: "I'm here."

LAGARDÈRE: I'm here. (low) That's Nevers' motto.

GONZAGUE: As you don't have the voice of the one she's expecting, don't speak.

LAGARDÈRE: I will make a sign to her that we are spied on.

GONZAGUE: Precisely. She will deliver to you a bundle that you will take in silence and carry straight away to the Inn of Adam's Apple. In exchange you will have your fifty pistoles.

LAGARDÈRE: I am your man.

PEYROLLES: Hush! (in the distance the horn of an ox-cart is heard) That's the first signal. Nevers is approaching. On the second he will enter the forest.

GONZAGUE: Then my handsome cousin has no more than a quarter of an hour to live. Let's separate ourselves.

PEYROLLES: (to Lagardère) Your companions?

LAGARDÈRE: Here. (pointing to the back of the moat)

GONZAGUE: You remember the password?

LAGARDÈRE: I am here.

GONZAGUE: Till later. We will go back in through the small postern.

(They go back into the castle)

LAGARDÈRE: (tossing the purse away) Ah! God will take me to task in my last moments for not putting my sword into the torsos of those wretches! What to do now? Some infamy is being plotted around here! Let's go to the end. It's no longer a question of a duel, of scaling a ladder for love. But I intend to know. Here's the hour. Let's do what the Duke told me. No one. Ah! They are waiting for the password—I am here!

BLANCHE: (opening the window) God be praised! (she offers him her hand through the window.) I cannot see anything. Philippe, where are you?

LAGARDÈRE: Here! Let's be quick.

BLANCHE: I obey you, my Philippe. Here's our treasure; it's no longer safe with me.

LAGARDÈRE: (taking the bundle) Quick! Quick!

BLANCHE: Ah, I thought my heart was stronger.

LAGARDÈRE: Courage! Courage! (after having passed the child to Lagardère Blanche offers him a book) What's this?

BLANCHE: My book of hours; I've placed in it a hidden fold with your arms, and in this fold pages torn from the registry of Chaplain Don Bernard. (sound of a horn) A signal—. Save yourself, save yourself. (quickly pulling Lagardère's hand and pulling it to her lips) I love you! (she shuts the grill and disappears.)

LAGARDÈRE: What the devil is this? Ah, triple fool! What kind of adventure have I got myself into? Come on—make a good face over a bad hand! Sonofabitch! One can give him by the thousands to all the Light Cavalry. I wager a thousand pistoles and from the devil—that not a single one would guess what I'm holding in my arms at this moment. Ah, what a white and rosy child he is! How he sleeps. Ah, my word, he's very cute. You are cute, Miss or Mister—but very embarrassing. Fight then, with this in my arms. If I leave, Nevers will come and they'll kill him. I don't want him killed. No—by a thousand devils, I don't want it. Ah, yet another signal. That one's just been given quite near us. And despite what I said the assassins are following him and watching him, no question. Which direction is he coming from?

NEVERS: (descending the stairs) Two torch bearers wouldn't be bad here.

LAGARDÈRE: Someone—it's Nevers. Yes, it's him. Over here, Duke.

NEVERS: (unsheathing) You are Lagardère: To work, Chevalier, I'm in a hurry. Just touch swords with me so that I know where you are.

LAGARDÈRE: Not before you've listened to me.

NEVERS: (groping towards him) Some further insult against Miss de Caylus?

LAGARDÈRE: No, by Jove! I was unaware. Be very careful.

NEVERS: There has to be blood.

LAGARDÈRE: Listen to me.

NEVERS: No, no—

LAGARDÈRE: Ah, devil from Hell! Is it necessary to crack your skull to prevent you from killing your child?

NEVERS: My child! My daughter?

LAGARDÈRE: Ah, it's a girl! Eh, by Jove, here she is.

NEVERS: My daughter, in your arms!

LAGARDÈRE: Softly—you are going to wake her up.

NEVERS: At least tell me—

LAGARDÈRE: Devil of a man—he won't even let me speak. Here he is trying to force me to tell him stories! Look, hold this for me, daddy. Gently, very gently. There, there—enough hugs, papa We are already two old friends, the little one and me. Let's put her down—first of all these bundles of hay. (placing the child on the hay)

NEVERS: Ah, Chevalier!

LAGARD: (with nobility) Now, I will answer for her on my life, Duke, I expiate, as much as is in me, a double insult—to you first of all who are honesty itself! and to her mother who is a noble wife.

NEVERS: You've seen Miss de Caylus?

LAGARDÈRE: I've seen Madame de Nevers.

NEVERS: Where's that?

LAGARDÈRE: At this window.

NEVERS: And it was she who confided to you?

LAGARDÈRE: This treasure? Yes, thinking she was giving it to yourself. Oh, don't try to understand. Strange things are happening here, Duke, and since you are in a mood to fight, By Jove you will soon have a joyous heart.

NEVERS: An attack?

LAGARDÈRE: An assassination! Ordered by a man I don't know but who's called Milord, and who calls himself your cousin.

NEVERS: Gonzague! A friend, almost a brother!. Ah, Chevalier, it's not possible!

LAGARDÈRE: (polishes his sword) I don't know if that is possible—but I know quite well what this is. And, as I don't think you are in the mood to flee before assassins—

NEVERS: No, by Jove! I will await them if only to know who the bandit is that's paying them

LAGARDÈRE: (to his sword) You hear, my beauty. Ah, that's enough of escapades! Praise God, Miss. Let's try to distinguish ourselves and to be led by a noble girl—

NEVERS: You are going to fight for me?

LAGARDÈRE: A bit for you. Immensely for the little one.

NEVERS: Ah, Lagardère, I didn't know you; you are a great heart.

LAGARDÈRE: As for me, I'm a fool! But, Bah! The child has transformed me, turned me inside out. I think I'm going to be good and well behaved now—Hush! (he listens)

NEVERS: What is it?

LGARDERRE: They are crawling up there.

NEVERS: Wait—it's Charot, my page. Who ought to be waiting for me at the inn and who must have followed me. (the page is seen descending the stairway on the left.)

LAGARDÈRE: It's him. This way, little fellow.

PAGE: You are surrounded, Milord, lost!

LAGARDÈRE: Bah! There are only eight of them.

PAGE: There are twenty. When they learned there are two of you, they added reinforcements.

LAGARDÈRE: Do you think you can slip out of here?

PAGE: Yes.

LAGARDÈRE: Run to the inn. Jump on my horse, and find my volunteers who are in the hamlet of Cernay. Tell them, "Lagardère is in danger." Are you ready?

PAGE: Yes.

LAGARDÈRE: You are a brave little chap. (pointing to the stairway) Kill my horse, but get there, little one, get there. (The page vanishes)

NEVERS: (pointing) Watch out, Chevalier, I see a sword shining down there.

LAGARDÈRE: Do as I do, Duke, and quickly. (he pulls the cart and aided by the Duke, they hastily improvise a barricade using bales of hay.)

NEVERS: Chevalier, henceforth between us it's life and death; if I live all is common between us—if I live.

LAGARDÈRE: Bah! You won't die—

NEVERS: If I die, my daughter needs a protector—

LAGARDÈRE: Well, on my place in paradise, I will be her protector.

NEVERS: My brother!

LAGARDÈRE: To our swords. Here they come.

(The assassins approach from two directions. Cocardasse and Passepoil from the breach at the right. Staupitz and the bullies from the rear. Still others by the left.)

LAGARDÈRE: I'll watch over the child. Don't show yourself too much.

STAUPITZ: There he is.

NEVERS: Yes, it's me. I'm here.

STAUPITZ: Just Nevers?

LAGARDÈRE: Lagardère, also, my wise guys.

COCARDASSE: Sonofabitch! The Parisian is in it. Do like me, littler one, push, my pebble, push. (The circle is narrowed but they seem hesitant to strike the first blow.)

NEVERS: Well, cowardly assassins, you don't dare to come forward.

LAGARDÈRE: They will need pikes to make a hole in our breasts.

STAUPITZ: Forward: (First skirmish. With the support of their fortifications they repulse the first assault.)

LAGARDÈRE: (pushing his sword.) Here's for you, Staupitz; Yours, Saldagne. (wounding them both)

PASSEPOIL: He's superb to watch from a distance.

COCARDASSE: Alert, the rest of you. We are going to have a real battle. Here are the King's volunteers; I unbutton for them.

LAGARDÈRE: (calling) Help Lagardère, my braves, help Lagardère.

CARRIGUE: (in the distance) Here we are, Captain, here we are.

(He appears with his men and enters the moat through the breach)

NEVERS: Forward, Lagardère. Let's charge.

LAGARDÈRE: Charge!

(They emerge from their fortification and charge in their turn. Gonzague, masked, sword in hand can be seen hanging back at the side.)

NEVERS: Clumsy bunch!

GONZAGUE: Neither Philippe nor this Lagardère must leave this place alive.

LAGARDÈRE: Victory! (he makes the bandits retreat)

FAENZA: Get Nevers!

NEVERS: I am here. (wounding him)

GONZAGUE: This has got to stop. (plunging his sword into Nevers' back)

NEVERS: Ah, help me, Lagardère, help me!

LAGARDÈRE: Here I am. (with his redoubtable sword, he attacks Gonzague while while Carrigue and his volunteers protect him from Gonzague.) Assassin! I haven't seen your face, but I will recognize you anywhere.

(Lagardère strikes him with his sword in the right hand, and the pain causes the sword to drop from Gonzague's hand.)

NEVERS: (to Lagardère) Gonzague—my daughter. Brother, avenge me. Save her. (he falls)

LAGARDÈRE: (going to Nevers) Dead!

ALL: Dead!

LAGARDÈRE: (taking the child and pointing to the stairway at the left) Nevers is dead. Long live Nevers!

(he rapidly climbs the stairs to the bridge.)

GONZAGUE: Nevers' daughter—a thousand pistoles to the one that captures her.

LAGARDÈRE: (reaching the head of the bridge) Come find her behind my sword. Your hand will bear my mark, and when the time comes, you won't come to Lagardère, Lagardère will come to you.

CURTAIN

ACT I
SCENE 3

The interior of an armorer's shop. A door at the rear opening on a street. A door to the right, near the audience, also opening outside. Door to the left leading to the interior. Attached to the wall, masks, suits of armor, gauntlets, trophies. Windows in cutaway to the right. In front of the window a work bench.

TONIO: The señorita will not be late. Vespers is just ringing. If master Henríquez had permitted me to leave as well, I would have seen in the square this little gypsy that all our hidalgos are so crazy about—and they will end by skipping out one fine day, that troupe of gypsies that she enriches with her dancing and her singing.

COACARDASSE: (entering noisily) Holá! Sonofabitch! Isn't there anybody in this barracks?

(Cocardasse is dressed richly as a matador.)

TONIO: Señor Caballero, I am at your orders.

COCARDASSE: Hey, in that case, get over here, rascal! Does anyone know how to polish-a rapier in your casern?

TONIO: Certainly.

COCARDASSE Well! Polish this one a bit to demonstrate. (pulling an enormous sword from his scabbard)

TONIO: Why, how long it is!

COCARDASSE: (to the apprentice who wants to take the blade) Hey, Fighter! No one touches this except with respect, and, this blade, as you see, has touched more breasts than you have hair on your skull. Never has it missed its man. Goddam!

TONIO: Never!

COCARDASSE: Never!

TONIO: Oh! How rusty!

COCARDASSE: You call this rust? kiddo—it's blood!

TONIO: Blood!

COCARDASSE: What do you want? This crazy Petronella—Petronella's what I call her in memory of a duchess who honored me with some bounties! Petronella cannot keep still when someone irritates her lord and master. She quivers from guard to blade tip; she rushes out of her scabbard by herself— And once she's in play she touches, and when she touches, she kills.

TONIO: Often?

COCARDASSE: Always.

TONIO: Truly?

COCARDASSE: Eh, fighter, you doubt it? Petronella, my darling, they doubt you. Hey, heavens, she's going to find you all by herself. Where do you want her to touch you? Where do you want her to kill you? (pushing thrusts)

Ah, ah, ah!

TONIO: (recoiling) But I don't doubt, I don't doubt. Give me your Petronella. I'll return it to you shining like a ray of sunshine—fine blade.

COCARDASSE: I really believe it. Petronella has no equal.

TONIO: Oh, we have a better here.

COCARDASSE: Come on! Show me a little—

TONIO: (pointing to a rapier on the wall) Look.

COCARDASSE: (not looking at first) Petronella doesn't recognize a sword better than herself—- but that one is the first one in the world. You don't have it in your scrap-iron, little fellow. (then looking) Oh, Sonofabitch! I'm not mistaken—that sword.

TONIO: It belongs to Master Henríquez.

COCARDASSE: (aside) Oh, that's really it! Sonofabitch! Lagardère is here, or Lagardère is dead. (without listening to Tonio) This Henríquez is not from this country?—-Will you answer, fighter!

TONIO: No. He came here three years ago.

COCARDASSE: Three years ago? With a little girl?

TONIO: Yes.

COCARDASSE: And he came?

TONIO: From Pamplona, I think.

COCARDASSE (aside) It's him, my little Parisian! Oh, then we must keep one eye open, as in Burgos, as in Seville, as in Pamplona—I will return, and this time I will allow myself to be seen. I will again speak to this ingrate whose name alone shakes my heart—Sonofabitch! Since I lost Passepoil, this Lagardère is my only love. (aloud) Au-revoir. (he leaves)

TONIO: There's a proud matador.

BLANCHE: (entering hastily) Tonio!

TONIO: (turning) Huh? The señorita!

BLANCHE: (uneasily) Lock that door.

TONIO: (locking it) Right away. You seem frightened?

BLANCHE: Wrongly, no doubt. It seems to me someone was following me. I hurried my errand and thanks to heaven I am returned. (knocking at the small door)

BLANCHE: (terrified) Don't open.

WOMAN'S VOICE: (outside) Have no fear.

TONIO: (looking through the keyhole) It's a young girl, a gypsy. (looking again) Should I send her away?

BLANCHE: No!

TONIO: (opening) Come in!

FLOR: (gaily) Thanks! (she's a gypsy and holds a Basque drum [tambourine] in her hand; looking at Blanche) I was very sure I wasn't mistaken.

TONIO: What is it you want with us, infidel?

FLOR: Just now, as she crossed the square, the señora dropped this silver coin in my tambourine.

TONIO: Well, gypsies never refuse money.

FLOR: No, but when they are honest girls they want to earn it. For this money, I will tell the señora, the past, the present, and the future.

BLANCHE: (moving away) That's unnecessary.

TONIO: Begone, devil's daughter. The señora doesn't want to listen to anything.

FLOR: But if I am speaking to her of Flor?

BLANCHE: (stopping) Of Flor? Flor—it's you! you!

FLOR: Yes, I've grown, and I am less ugly.

TONIO: Ugly! This little infidel is very pretty.

FLOR: I recognized you immediately and I followed you. Because I need you to say "My little Flor, I still love you and I forgive you."

BLANCHE: Eh! What do I have to forgive you for?

FLOR: My ingratitude. You sheltered me and you treated me like you sister, he, like a daughter. But I was obliged to live like you as a recluse. Not to see the Sun except through a blind that was always closed. And for me it's necessary to have space, air, liberty. One day I saw Nathaniel pass, the leader of the tribe that had adopted me; the evening of that day, I left you—you, my good angel.

BLANCHE: Oh, I forgive you. Because I am really happy to see you again. Tonio, you can leave us.

TONIO: (to Flor) Cursed girl! Do you know if little Pepita who will surely be damned like you is dancing today in the square of the Inquisition?

FLOR: Yes, a new dance. There's already a crowd. I warn you of that.

TONIO: Oh, I will make a place for myself. (he leaves running)

FLOR: You will allow me to remain a few minutes with you?

BLANCHE: I beg you to. They are lucky, those who have companions to confide the fullness of their souls to. Pain or joy. Me, I'm alone, always alone.

FLOR: And him?

BLANCHE: What can I say of him? He asks nothing of me.

FLOR: Well, chat with me, dear sister, like when we were little. Tell me what you have learned of your destiny. Because between you and me, I am no more a sorceress than you are. And you will know what I know of the past, present, and future when I tell you I loved you before, I love you today and I will always love you. (she kisses Blanche)

BLANCHE: What do I know myself? I think I was born in

France. I'm unaware even of my age. Where I see light for the first time, it's in the Spanish Pyrenees. There I kept the goats of mountain folk who gave us hospitality. Later, my friend was afraid of being pursued, so we quickly changed residence, and he himself changed his name.

FLOR: Indeed, in the past he called himself Don Luis, and today, this boy called him Henríquez.

BLANCHE: His true name is Henri de Lagardère, and that's how I've known him. We were at Burgos for more than a year. In the middle of the night someone woke me gently. It was him. "Get up, quick, child, we must flee, they have discovered our tracks." "Who?" "You have enemies."

FLOR: You have enemies? You?

BLANCHE: Well, terrible ones, you are going to see. They were already climbing the stairs. They were going to open the door. Henri replaced the absent bar with his arm. "Child," he said to me, "you are brave and you will do what I tell you." "Yes." "Tie your curtains to the window and let yourself slip into the garden. Will you do it?" "Yes, if you promise to join me." "I promise you." I did what he ordered me to do. Hardly in the garden, I shouted to him, "I'm here." "And I am, too," he replied in a dazzling voice. "I am here." And I heard in the room I'd just left, the clashing of swords, blasphemies, and the voice of my friend dominating all this uproar, and repeating ceaselessly, "I am here, Lagardère, Lagardère!" I heard two terrible screams, as two bodies fell on the floor. From terror, I closed my eyes. When I opened them, my friend was next to me; he took me in his arms, and carried me away, still shouting, "Lagardère, Lagardère!"

FLOR: I will never forget that name.

BLANCHE: To Seville, to Pamplona, the same care to hide me, the same dangers, the same flight. For three years we were in Segovia, and our enemies appeared to have lost our track, or to have forgotten us. And yet, I'm afraid. Yes, I am afraid for Henri forbids me to go out to see anyone, he increases his watchfulness and precaution. All this, I understand plainly, is the danger of former times that is returning.

FLOR: (smiling) Isn't it rather jealousy that's beginning?

BLANCHE: Jealousy?

FLOR: Can he see you and not love you? If he loves you, can he not be jealous? At present, tell me, your friend Lagardère—is he still handsome, still proud, still good? Look, don't blush so much, and confess everything, in a whisper—you still love him?

BLANCHE: Why in a whisper?

FLOR: As loud as you like.

BLANCHE: Yes, I love him.

FLOR: Right. And he's told you twenty time, a hundred times, that he adores you.

BLANCHE: Him? He loves me, but like his daughter.

FLOR: At his age? Come on, that's impossible.

BLANCH: Impossible? Why?

FLOR: Why? Listen, sis, if your Lagardère isn't madly in love with you—then—

BLANCHE: Then?

FLOR: Then he's in love with someone else.

BLANCHE: Someone else? (uproar outside. Tonio enters very frightened and locks the door at the back behind him.)

FLOR: What's going on?

TONIO: They are fighting, they are killing each other in the square of the Inquisition because of you, or rather your comrade—

FLOR: Diavolina! Why?

TONIO: Ah, I don't know why. I received two punches. I didn't ask anymore.

BLANCHE: And Henri has not returned. If he found himself in the midst of battle.

TONIO: By chance he left without arms today.

BLANCHE: Without arms.

HENRI: (outside) Holá, Tonio!

BLANCHE: His voice! It's his voice!

TONIO: He will scold me for having let this little damnation in.

FLOR: I'm leaving; I want to know what's going on. But we will see each other again soon. (low) We will talk about him again. Till later. (to Tonio who wants to open the side door) Oh, it's unnecessary, I know the way. (She leaves; Blanche has gone to the door of her room.)

BLANCHE (aside) If he were to be in love with someone else. Oh, I'm going to find out.

TONIO: (who's gone to the door at the back) Go quickly, Señora, the master is not alone. (Blanche goes in quickly)

(Henri enters supported slightly by Chaverny whose costume is in disorder. Henri holds in his hand the truncheon of Chaverny's sword.)

CHAVERNY: Praise God, my master, Even at Versailles, I don't know your equal to play at swords, but you had in your hand only one poor blade already broken in the mêlée.

HENRI: Tonio, quick—a glass of Alicante for this gentleman.

CHAVERNY: Oh, I'm getting better, but I still feel worn out from the blow of a stick that I received. A terrible blow, my word, which, after breaking my sword that I was trying to protect myself with, almost broke my skull. The cowards! The bandits! Hum! To kill with a dagger blow passes still, but with a blow from a stick. Yuck! It's ignoble!

HENRI: Those wretched gypsies are not even Christians; they have neither faith nor law. What were you going to do in such bad company?

CHAVERNY: Why have those wise guys got such pretty girls?

TONIO: (bringing wine) Your Excellency means to speak of Pepita.

CHAVERNY: Yes, she's the most spicy creature! Alas, I swear indeed to steal her from them; that little honey would go marvelously at the Opera. (looking around him) Ah, where have you led me, my master? To an armorer's, I guess.

HENRI: You're at my place.

CHAVERNY: Truly! Then, my brave, quickly replace this parade sword for me.

HENRI: Tonio, choose what we have of the finest and best tempered. And now, sir, would you indeed taste my wine?

CHAVERNY: It's excellent, but I won't finish this glass, except in drinking your health. (they clink). You must have been a soldier.

HENRI: Yes.

CHAVERNY: You are not Spanish.

HENRI: No.

CHAVERNY: I wager you are French.

HENRI: And Parisian.

CHAVERNY: Shake. We are fellow countrymen, as good folks say. (pouring him a drink) The name's Chaverny.

HENRI: The Marquis de Chaverny.

CHAVERNY: Yes, and you?

HENRI: Allow me not to tell you my name. You understand and you will pardon my discretion when I tell you I am proscribed.

CHAVERNY: Proscribed! The Devil! You must have got mixed up in some conspiracy. That of Castellmare, right?

HENRI: If you like.

CHAVERNY: You are a gentleman?

HENRI: King Louis XIV made me a chevalier.

CHAVERNY: Praise God! If he'd seen your demeanor just now in the midst of that band of demons, he would have made you a count at least; and as for me, I owe you my life. I would make you rich if I were not ruined.

HENRI: You were, I think, a cousin of Philippe, Duke de Nevers?

CHAVERNY: Yes, yes, I am richly connected; I am still cousin of Philippe de Gonzague, who passes rightly for a Croesus. And if he dies without heir I will be his inheritor.

HENRI: Hasn't he any children?

CHAVERNY: Legitimate, no. And he never will have.

HENRI: He's still married?

CHAVERNY: Yes, with Miss Blanche de Caylus.

HENRI: Widow of Philippe de Nevers.

CHAVERNY: Ah! ah! You know that scandal?

HENRI: Up to the moment when Nevers' widow consented to exchange her name for that of Gonzague.

CHAVERNY: That's all? Then you don't know the most curious adventure.

HENRI: Truly?

CHAVERNY: Gonzague will never be a father because he's never been married.

HENRI: Ah!

CHAVERNY: Blanche was forced to obey Mr. de Caylus and wed Prince Gonzague; but before she proudly admitted to him her secret marriage with the deceased Nevers.

HENRI: Cowardly murdered.

CHAVERNY: On orders of Mr. de Caylus.

HENRI: Ah, they told you that?

CHAVERNY: Yes, moreover, Blanche declared that a daughter was born to this marriage and must inherit the immense fortune of her father to the detriment of Philippe de Gonzague. My fine cousin nobly recognized legally the rights of this child. The wealth was sequestered until the day when the daughter of Nevers who was carried off by the murderer of her father shall be found, or at least until the hour that the death of this child is actually duly verified. Finally, Philippe de Gonzague engages on his honor as a gentleman not to be the spouse of Blanche de Caylus except in name, and never to cross the sill of the Princess's door, thus condemning himself to neither the one nor the other of the two treasures; it's much better to be like me, poor and a bachelor.

HENRI: Blanche de Caylus has then not forgotten Philippe de Nevers?

CHAVERNY: She hasn't stopped wearing mourning for her first husband. Her room is furnished with souvenirs of him, and she places her prie-dieu beneath Nevers' picture.

HENRI: How then has she forgotten her daughter?

CHAVERNY: She believes her dead, and sees with terror the approach of her fifteenth year of widowhood.

HENRI: Why?

CHAVERNY: Because at the end of fifteen years, her husband can assemble a family tribunal to decide for him if the rights of the absent have lapsed, and that her mother must enter into her inheritance.

HENRI: Which will then fall into the hands of Gonzague.

CHAVERNY: He's counting on it, but he wasn't counting on his wife or on me.

HENRI: On you?

CHAVERNY: Yes. Without me, who am like him cousins with Nevers in an inferior degree, it's true; but the Princess who appears to cordially detest her spouse told me six months ago, "You were, you are a good relative, a true friend of Philippe de Nevers. If God has taken my daughter from me, it's to you I will leave her father's inheritance."

HENRI: To you.

CHAVERNY: I have many opportunities. They thought to follow the tracks of the ravisher of the child. To the frontiers of Spain. The Princess rushed, looked everywhere, promising her fortune to whoever would return her daughter to her. But her numerous emissaries have learned nothing. Then I said to myself—

HENRI: That the inheritance would come to you?

CHAVERNY: Yes, if I were not more clever than the others. And, on that, I left, determined to investigate Spain in its deepest recesses. If Nevers' daughter is in this country, I swear to God I will find her—and when I've found her—

HENRI: What will you do?

CHAVERNY: You are a French gentleman, and you are asking me what I will do? Sonofabitch! I will take the child back to her mother. Which will cost me something like fifteen or twenty millions. It will be a madness, I agree. But I am sure of never reproaching myself for it.

HENRI: (taking his hand) Fine, fine—you are truly blood of Nevers.

TONIO: Sir, here's you sword. The King of France does not have a better.

CHAVERNY: Unfortunately, I cannot pay for it like a king. Still, I—

HENRI: Sir, would you do me the honor of accepting this sword, and promise me to wear it in memory of the proscribed.

CHAVERNY: Chevalier, I am unable to refuse you! Only you will permit me to pay the day's wages of this brave lad. (he tosses his purse. Four o'clock strikes.)

TONIO: A full purse!

CHAVERNY: Four o'clock. (aside) La Pepita must be waiting for me behind the old Cathedral. (aloud) Chevalier, I am forced to leave you. We will meet again, I hope. At least once. Shake! Except against the Regent this sword will be completely yours, everywhere and always.

HENRI: Everywhere and always? Perhaps I'll remind you of that fine oath.

CHAVERNY: God watch over you and protect you. (he leaves)

(Tonio escorts Chaverny to the door; Henri falls into a seat near the table)

HENRI: (to himself) Nevers' widow has respected his memory. Blanche's mother weeps for her. Why did he inform me of this? What to do now? Oh, I don't know, I don't know, any more. This mother has rights. She weeps and demands her child from god, while, as for me I no longer have any! No. These sacred rights cannot be purchased even at the price of life. I've given my life, it's true. What am I owed for that? Nothing, nothing! (Blanche enters quietly, and with a gesture sends Tonio away, who leaves shutting the door behind him. Henri turns at the rustling noise of her dress as she approaches.)

HENRI: Who's coming here?

BLANCHE: Me, my friend. You were alone and I thought I might come in. I see you so rarely.

HENRI: And you accuse me—

BLANCHE: God prevent me from it. I suffer sometimes, it's true, when I am alone. When I see you I no longer suffer. I am happy.

HENRI: Yes, you have a daughter's tenderness for me.

BLANCHE: But don't you have a father's tenderness for me?

HENRI: Me? (he wants to get away from her)

BLANCHE: Oh, don't leave me already. No. Rather come sit down near me. (she makes him sit in an armchair and takes her place on a stool) It's been a long time since we've chatted. In the old days time passed quickly when we were together as we are now—

HENRI: The hours no longer belong to us.

BLANCHE: Why? (he deflects his eyes) Henri, if you no longer want to speak to me—? Don't you want to see me any more? Ah, how you've changed since the day you told me, "You are not my daughter." You've really changed.

HENRI: (controlling himself) You're mistaken, Blanche. I had a beautiful dream, I was forgetting. I woke up, and I remember myself, that's all. I have a task to fulfill, the moment has come when my life is going to change, and I'm too old, my child, to start a new life.

BLANCHE: (smiling) Too old—

HENRI: At my age, others have a family.

BLANCHE: And you, my friend, you have only me.

HENRI: (forgetting himself) Only you! But for fifteen years you've been all my happiness.

BLANCHE: Really true?

HENRI: (controlling himself) When you no longer see me, will you think of me?

BLANCHE: (terrified) Are you going to leave me?

HENRI: Blanche, there's a brilliant life, a life of pleasures, of honors, of riches; the life of the lucky in this world and you do not know of it, dear child!

BLANCHE: What need have I to know it?

HENRI: You have to know it; you will have to make a choice, possibly. Today is your last day of doubt and ignorance—it's also my last day of youth and hope.

BLANCHE: Henri, in the name of heaven, explain yourself.

HENRI: Blanche, listen carefully. Consider carefully. Here we are—enjoying happiness or unhappiness all our lives. Reply to me with your conscience, with your heart.

BLANCHE: I will answer to you as to my father.

HENRI: Oh, not that name, never that name. My God! Perhaps it's the only one I've taught you to see in me, that you can see in me—a father.

BLANCHE: Henri!

HENRI: When I was a child, men of thirty were old geezers to me. How old do you think I am, Blanche?

BLANCHE: What do I care? I don't know your age, Henri, but the name I gave you just now, the name of father, I never say it without a smile.

HENRI: Why? I could be your father.

BLANCHE: As for me, Henri, I could not be your daughter.

HENRI: I was older than you are now when you came into the world. I was a man already.

BLANCHE: It's true since you were able to hold my cradle with one hand and your sword with the other.

HENRI: Dear child—don't look at me through your gratitude; see me as I am.

BLANCHE: (looking at him) I am looking at you, Henri. And I know nothing better in the world, nothing more noble, more handsome than you.

HENRI: You've always been happy with me?

BLANCHE: Yes, quite happy.

HENRI: And yet you told me that you suffered sometimes, and I've often made you weep. Why did you weep?

BLANCHE: Because of your absence, Henri—and then

HENRI: And then?

BLANCHE: Because of the thought that perhaps—

HENRI: Finish.

BLANCHE: That you love another woman.

HENRI: Oh, my God!

BLANCHE: And I would die of that!

HENRI: You love me then? Oh, but do you really know if you love me; do you know your heart?

BLANCHE: It is speaking and I am listening to it.

HENRI: If you ever have regrets—

BLANCHE: What regrets can I have if you remain by me?

HENRI: Listen. I already wanted to raise for you a corner of the curtain that hides you from the splendors of the world. Two months ago I took you to Madrid. You glimpsed the court, luxury. You heard the voices of the fests. Don't you feel yourself made for that life?

BLANCHE: Yes—with you.

HENRI: And without me?

BLANCHE: Nothing without you.

HENRI: You saw women, brilliant and adorned passing by—those women are happy, they have castles, mansions—

BLANCHE: When you are in our house, Henri, I prefer it to a palace.

HENRI: They have a family.

BLANCHE: You are my family.

HENRI: They have a mother.

BLANCHE: A mother! Now that's the only treasure I envy

them. After you, Henri, it's my mother that I think of most often. If I had a mother, Henri, if I heard her call you my son. Oh—what more joy could there be in paradise?

HENRI: And if you had to choose between your mother and me?

BLANCHE: Between my mother and you? Oh, Henri, Henri! I love you. I love you—(she hides her head in his breast)

HENRI: (with enthusiasm) God who sees us, who hears us, who judges us—then you are giving her to me? Oh, Blanche! Heaven—see the joy you are giving me. I am laughing, I'm weeping, I'm intoxicated, I'm crazy. Help me! Here you are all mine! My beloved! Don't pay attention to what I am saying. I am young, go—yes, I was lying. Those of my age are older than I am. Do you know why? The others are doing what I did before having encountered your cradle in my path. The others are squandering madly the treasure of their youth. You came—you, and I became avaricious to keep you all my soul, and I've never loved, I've never desired—and my heart that I allowed to sleep is awakening, and that heart is only twenty.

VOICE OF COCARDASSE: (off) Oh, don't be afraid, dear one. I have to speak to your master, dammit all.

HENRI: I recognize that voice! Oh, go in—quickly!

BLANCHE: Danger again?

HENRI: Of, don't be afraid. I am strong, I am invincible now. You love me, you love me! (he escorts her to the door to the interior, then seeing Cocardasse enter pushing Tonio in front of him. He leaps for his sword which he unhooks from the wall.)

COCARDASSE: Well, here he is, the master. I knew quite well he was here, dammit.

HENRI: Tonio, let this man in and go away. (Tonio leaves)

COCARDASSE (aside) Still proud! Still proud! He intends to run me through like the others. Attention.

HENRI: (going coldly to Cocardasse) There were eight of you in the moat of Caylus; eight cowardly assassins. How many of those wretches are still living?

COCARDASSE: Five died before their age, hit right there between the eyes. We recognized the boot of Nevers. Well, we are only three. Staupitz, Passepoil and myself.

HENRI: Don't count yourself. You are going to die.

COCARDASSE: Sonofabitch! You are quick like powder, but you will really take time to see. Petronella is at her toilette and I am unarmed.

HENRI: Come on. Are we lacking swords here? Choose!

COCARDASSE: Be unfaithful to Petronella? Never.

HENRI: Understand, old wise guy, that I do not intend to let you live now that you can see me and give me up as you sold and gave up Nevers. I swore not one of his murderers would escape me, and, after the eight valets, the master. Aren't you afraid of death?

COCARDASSE: To be killed by you? I would prefer living a hundred and ten years, ingrate. You suspect me, you, my brave pupil, my pride, my joy. Why, for you, Passepoil and I, we would be making a little fire grill. It's true, we are betraying someone, someone who paid us handsomely, to discover your hiding place, and that of the little one—that good Mr. de Peyrolles! We served him as he deserves. We had ferreted you out three times. In Burgos, In Seville, in Pamplona, and we had the delicacy of informing this excellent Mr. de Peyrolles, but only after a mysterious advice made you take to your heels.

HENRI: Those anonymous letters?

COCARDASSE: Were written by the hand of little apprentice Amable Passepoil, ex-clerk of the bailiwick of Falaise, his country. Alas, Passepoil will no longer write you. Orestes has lost his Pylades—the scamp has give in to the tumultuous torrent of his passion, and left me to follow an Andalusian Venus—small, dried up and so dark, I think she's a Negro. Oh, since Madame Eve women are the ruin of humanity; in short, when I discovered you were hereabouts, at the risk of a cut or two, I've come to warn you: Be on your guard! Peyrolles is in Segovia.

HENRI: Peyrolles!

COCARDASSE: In company of Staupitz!

HENRI: Staupitz.

COCARDASSE: They are not yet on your track, and Peyrolles despairs of ever finding you. The skinflint just cancelled my wages. He said to me, "I no longer need to seek this Lagardère; I've found the treasure he carried off."

HENRI: Blanche de Nevers! He's seen her?

COCARDASSSE: I was afraid like you, but Staupitz explained the thing to me. It seems it's very important to this good

Mr. de Peyrolles that Miss Blanche de Nevers be found and brought back to Paris by the end of this year. Despairing of finding the real one, Peyrolles will present a fake. And he's found one that will do, for he's leaving tonight for France. Staupitz has to meet him at the pass of the Devil's Tail—with mules.

HENRI: At what time?

COCARDASSE: At six o'clock.

HENRI: That's fine. Go away.

COCARDASSE: Is this all the friendship that you show me, you old Cocardasse? Have you forgotten that I made you who you are?

HENRI: You were in the moat at Caylus and you are still living. You see that I remember.

COCARDASSE: Sonofabitch! I'm not worth much, I know it, but on the salvation of my soul, neither I nor Passepoil touched Mr. de Nevers.

HENRI: On the salvation of your soul?

COCARDASSE: I swear it.

HENRI: (offering him his hand) Fine.

COCARDASSE: Oh, doggone it, Now I can only ask one thing of you: the opportunity to get wounded for you.

HENRI: I can give you that.

COCARDASSE: Thanks, thanks!

HENRI: Meanwhile, you are going to do me a service. You will inquire for, you will find—in the town a French gentleman by name of Chaverny. You will deliver this letter to him. (he writes) "Marquis, you can return to Paris; Miss de Nevers is en route to France."

COCARDASSE: Is there a response?

HENRI: No. you told me at the Pass of the Devil's Tail at six o'clock?

COCARDASSE: Yes, Staupitz has to bring mules and watch over them. Hurry, my little fellow. When will I see you again?

HENRI: Soon!

COCARDASSE: Where?

HENRI: In France—in Paris!

COCARDASSE: Oh, dammit! You are putting your head in the wolf's throat.

HENRI: I told you—After the valets, the master. And the time has come.

(At a gesture from Henri Cocardasse leaves, bowing. The Curtain falls.)

CURTAIN

ACT I
SCENE 4

A mountainous view.

At rise, a gypsy ballet.

CHAVERNY: (after the ballet) Son of Egypt, thanks to my doubloons, peace is made between us. And you've given me a dance for my money. But Pepita wouldn't refuse me a little song in the patois of her country. Come on, my charmer.

PEPITA: I can refuse nothing to you. (sings a Spanish song. After the song, the ballet resumes. Then, after the ballet)

CHAVERNY: My friends, to seal our reconciliation, by my orders a light meal awaits you. Whoever's thirsty, follow me.

(Everyone leaves with Chaverny, except a few women who want to drag Passepoil with them, but he disengages himself and remains alone)

PASSEPOIL: Go drink with those men? Fool around with those women? No, no! Oh, women, women! The sight of a mantilla drives me mad, furious, enraged. It reminds me of my perfidious one, my ingrate, my traitress! I, Amable Passepoil, the third sword in Europe, I'm being modest, I think I'm actually the second, me—sacrificed to whom? To an apothecary! Yuck! And I've been unable to turn his body into a sieve, a spittoon. No, he fled, the coward, and I've spent my last doubloon pursuing him, and my last sou. Ah, Passepoil, my child—what's life without love and without a sou? Nothing! But how to finish with her? If I hanged myself? If I frowned myself? No, all that disfigures. Hey, someone's coming. Who's coming there? Hum! It's a proud cavalier. Oh, if I can pick a quarrel with him, I won't have the trouble of killing myself.

COCARDASSE: (to himself) Damn, it wasn't easy to find that Marquis. Still, he's got Lagardère's letter. Hey, who's this character? A spy of Peyrolles' perhaps? Oh, Sonofabitch. He's a monument. If I brush one of his pilasters to see? Hey, there!

PASSEPOIL: Let's give him a strong prod.

COCARDASSE: (pushing him away) Sonofabitch!

PASSEPOIL: Son of a whore!

COCARDASSE: Forward, Petronella.

PASSEPOIL: On guard!

COCARDASSE: (recognizing him) Hey, there—

PASSEPOIL: Cocardasse!

COCARDASSE: Ah, my pebble!

PASSEPOIL: Say that you forgive me.

COCARDASSE: Could Orestes have it in for his Pylades? No.

Receive your pardon in this embrace. You're returning to me, ingrate, like a prodigal child.

PASSEPOIL: I did nothing, neither here nor there.

COCARDASSE: And we lost our wages on account of Peyrolles, who's given up searching for Lagardère.

PASSEPOIL: Who we never would have found.

COCARDASSE: Hush—as for me, I saw him.

PASSEPOIL: That little Parisian?

COCARDASSE: Yes.

PASSEPOIL: Oh, the dear child. And he didn't kill you?

COCARDASSE: We've made peace. But still, brave as a Caesar, he's returning to Paris, and you understand, my pebble, that where Lagardère goes, we are going.

PASSEPOIL: Oh, yes, I love him, that little fellow. It's necessary that I keep loving

COCARDASSE: Only, to go to Paris, we need money, and I don't have any.

PASSEPOIL: As for me, it's no different. I don't have any

COCARDASSE: Have no fear, my pebble, Peyrolles will pay the expenses of our voyage.

PASSEPOIL: That good Mr. Peyrolles is here. He's a great rogue, and I have a presentiment that he'll end badly. Oh, that good Mr. Peyrolles. It's he, I see him coming down there, in bad enough company.

(Peyrolles enters with Nathaniel)

PEYROLLES: We've come to an agreement on our facts. Yesterday evening you signed the declaration prepared and received the agreed upon sum. Now, name the young girl.

NATHANIEL: That's fair.

PASSEPOIL: A young girl for Mr. de Peyrolles. O love! Then you really are for all ages.

COCARDASSE: Hush! I'm going to tell you the thing.

NATHANIEL: Flor! Flor!

PEYROLLES: Six o'clock! Staupitz ought to be at the pass with the mules.

FLOR: (entering) You are calling me, Master?

NATHANIEL: Yes. To tell you goodbye.

FLOR: Goodbye?

NATHANIEL: You are going to leave the tribe, leave Spain.

FLOR: Leave you?

PEYROLLES: To go to France, to kiss a mother who's been weeping for you for the last fifteen years.

FLOR: A mother! I have a mother?

PEYROLLES: Rich, and noble. You will have a palace,

diamonds. You will go to court.

FLOR: To Court!

PEYROLLES: In a week we'll be in Paris.

FLOR: In Paris!

PEYROLLES: Holá! Someone call Staupitz and have him bring the mules here.

COCARDASSE: Present, Mr. de Peyrolles.

PEYROLLES: You jokers haven't been hanged yet?

COCARDASSE: Always a little joke. We knew you were going to return to France; the highways are not safe. You will need an escort.

PEYROLLES: Only to the frontier. Lead in Staupitz.

PASSEPIL: Right away. (he and Cocardasse leave)

PEYROLLES: We are going to leave.

FLOR: At least give me time to say goodbye to those who were a family to me.

PEYROLLES: So be it, but be quick!

PEPITA: You're leaving?

FLOR: Yes, I am going to France, to Paris.

PEPITA: We will see each other then. They're taking you this evening; tonight they are carrying me off.

FLOR: You!

PEPITA: Silence!

PEYROLLES: Well?

PASSEPOIL: The mules have been taken!

PEYROLLES: Taken! And Staupitz who was guarding them.

PEYROLLES: Dead!

COCARDASSE: They're bringing him in.

NATHANIEL: Look—is this really the man that was with you?

PEYROLLES: Yes—yes, it's Staupitz, Staupitz who's been struck down like the others—the same hand has given him the blow!

COCARDASSE: A thousand devils! Lagardère has been through here.

FLOR: Lagardère!

CURTAIN

ACT II
SCENE 5

The nest of Medor.

A vast and rich gallery on the ground floor of Gonzague's hotel in Paris. Glazed doors at the back giving on the garden. Side doors.

ARCHITECT: And quick, trace the work for tomorrow, it's a question of transforming this gallery as they have already transformed the courtyard, the gardens. Distribute everything in compartments of four square feet each, and number those compartments.

(The workers measure and attach numbers to the walls on the right and left.)

COCARDASSE: (arriving from the rear) Have no fear! Enter with a firm tread, my pebble. And raise your head, so as to lower it to all these flunkeys—

PASSEPOIL: Where are you taking me?

COCARDASSE: For the month we've been in Paris we've lived on our Spanish doubloons. Yesterday, we spent our last. Now, it's a question of reestablishing our finances, and, as you told me this morning, this good Mr. de Peyrolles forbade his door to you—well, then! I've brought you to Mr. Gonzague's himself who will perhaps be less insolent than his lackey of an intendant. I've taken my information. Mr. Gonzague is rich to millions of millions. The Regent who wishes him well granted him a monopoly of shares against merchandise; it's as if he had granted him a mountain of gold.

PASSEPOIL: I don't understand.

COCARDASSE: You going to understand. A share in a company of the Indies, otherwise known as the Mississippi is a piece of paper which is—

PASSEPOIL: Worth nothing.

COCARDASSE: Eh, dammit. That rag is a hundred times more precious than metal. To have it, men are giving their lands, their châteaux. The women give everything—and even a little more. Do you see what these workers are doing? They are marking out the compartments where vendors of this paper will be established.

ARCHITECT: (marking) Number 935, 936, 937. You are measuring very carefully. Remember, that down there every strip of ground is worth gold.

COCARDASSE: (to Passepoil) He's right. I permitted myself to say that. At rue Quincampoix a little hunchback no bigger than this had won a million five hundred thousand pounds, only to loan his hump to use as a writing stand. He retired yesterday, and sold his funds to anther hunchback who's getting rich like him.

PASSEPOIL: Son of a whore! That makes one despair of being handsome and well built! But, since everything costs so much nowadays that can be valued, and pointed or elongated properly, skillfully—

COCARDASSE: (low) It's that I've just got to know Mr. de Gonzague himself.

ARCHITECT: There still remain two and a half feet—false measure.

COCARDASSE: (to Passepoil) That will be for a skinny man. (great uproar off) Let's not reveal ourselves right away. (they go into an opening) Ah, Mr. de Peyrolles—

(Peyrolles enters pushing back the crowd with his handkerchief; he's dressed richly, followed by a soliciting crowd.)

PEYROLLES: Look, look, gentlemen, hold yourselves at a distance, and don't forget the respect that is my due.

COCARDASSE: The rascal is superb!

SOLICITOR: I'm inscribing myself first to be in this place.

OTHERS: No, no—no favoritism.

PEYROLLES: Silence.

ALL: Hush! Listen!

PEYROLLES: The Counters of this gallery will be constructed and delivered tomorrow

ALL: (disappointed) Tomorrow!

SOLICITOR: I don't want to wait until tomorrow. I want to be inscribed right now.

ALL: Me, too. Me, too.

PEYROLLES: (pointing to Gonzague who enters) The Duke!

(Gonzague is followed by Chaverny, Navaille, and other gentlemen. All take off their hats and silence returns)

GONZAGUE: Hurry, Peyrolles.

NAVAILLE: Oh, fine faces!

PEYROLLES: (to Gonzague) They are white hot! They will pay any price you wish.

CHAVERNY: (laughing) Truly! Put the places up for auction. They will go very quickly and that will amuse us.

GONZAGUE: So be it. At auction. Go, gentlemen, set the example.

PEYROLLES: Gentlemen, the places are going to be auctioned.

NAVAILLE: Well, I begin. I offer five hundred pounds per month five square feet. (silence, aside) No one is going above that. Perhaps I've been a bit hasty.

SOLICITOR: (aside) To give five hundred pounds per month—forever

CHAVERNY: Bah! A thousand pounds per week

SOLICITOR: (low to others) They intend to exploit us.

GONZAGUE: (low) They are not whispering a word. What were you saying to me, Mr. de Peyrolles?

PEYROLLES: Gentlemen, these places are the last and the best. They will be given to the highest bidder. Let's see—number 927.

(silence)

CHAVERNY: (low) Fifteen hundred pounds.

NAVAILLE: That won't work, it's too much.

CHAVERNY: Not at all it's too cheap. (aloud) Two thousand five hundred.

SOLICITOR: (with effort) Three thousand.

PEYROLLES: (quickly) Sold!

CHAVERNY: The imbeciles!

PEYROLLES: 928.

CHAVERNY: Four thousand pounds.

NAVAILLE: (low) you are mad.

CHAVERNY: There are greater fools than me.

FIRST SOLICITOR: It's the same—

2nd SOLICITOR: I'll take it.

CHAVERNY: (low) What were you saying?

PEYROLLES: 929. Four thousand.

2nd SOLICITOR: Five thousand.

A WOMAM: Six thousand.

CHAVERNY: The women are getting involved. We are going to have a fine day.

2nd SOLICITOR: Seven thousand.

1st SOLICITOR : Eight thousand.

WOMAN: Ten thousand!

GONZAGUE: (low) There they are launched (aloud) Peyrolles, give it to Madame, we must be gallant. But you are not to give out any more now on a single place at less than twenty thousand pounds.

ALL: Twenty thousand pounds.

GONZAGUE: It's take it or leave it.

ALL: We'll take, we'll take it.

CHAVERNY For twenty thousand, and they were hesitating to give five hundred for them—

PEYROLLES Get yourselves inscribed and pay.

(The crowd surrounds Peyrolles and the secretary who inscribes them and receives the money.)

NAVAILLE: Here's the goldmine.

CHAVERNY: Hum! It's not sold, it's given. What a shame, cousin, that you don't have more places to rent.

COCARDASSE: (to Passepoil) He's right, these chickens would

have given all their feathers.

GONZAGUE: To the extent places are lacking, the fever increases. But nothing remains for me, nothing.

CHAVERNY: Look around carefully.

GONZAGUE: Ah, indeed. (laughing) I still have one place to rent.

ALL: What is it?

GONZAGUE: (laughing very hard) The kennel of Medor—of my dog.

ALL: (laughing) Ah, ah!

1st SOLICITOR: I've seen it, its is very habitable.

GONZAGUE: (laughing) But I won't give it up for less than ten thousand.

NAVAILLE: (laughing) A dog kennel!

A HUNCHBACK: (piercing the crowd) I'll take the doghouse for 30,000 pounds.

CHAVERNY: Bravo! You know the value of things. You appear to me to be a bold and adroit speculator.

HUNCHBACK: Bold, yes. Adroit enough, we will see?

ALL: Fine! Bravo!

PEYROLLES: Friend, you pay in cash you know.

HUNCHBACK: I know. There's your money in beautiful and good notes.

COCARDASSE: (to Passepoil) Have we ever known a hunchback, my pebble?

PASSEPOIL: (disdainfully) Never!

COCARDASSE: Praise God! Still, I've seen those eyes somewhere.

HUNCHBACK: My receipt?

PEYROLLES: That's fair. (he signs)

HUNCHBCK: Good business. I am here.

GONZAGUE: (turning excitedly) Huh! You said?

HUNCHBACK: Milord, I said that I am here for a week at my place, and I will try to use my time profitably.

GONZAGUE: What's your name?

HUNCHBACK: Aesop.

GONZAGUE: Huh?

HUNCHBACK: Aesop.

NAVAILLE: That's not a Christian name.

HUNCHBACK: It's a hunchback's name.

NAVAILLE: And a villainous name.

ALL: (laughing) To your kennel!

(The crowd leaves with the hunchback in its midst.)

HUNCHBACK: (to Navaille) You find me ugly, right? I was even uglier before. It's the privilege of ugliness, the years use it as beauty; you lose, I win. In fifty years we'll all be alike. (he leaves)

COCARDASSE: (to Passepoil) My pebble, it's now or never to make ourselves seen—You are hesitating?

PASSEPOIL: I'm timid in society.

COCARDASSE: Well, I will go first.

CHAVERNY: (noticing them) Look there, gentlemen. It's the day of masquerades. The hunchback wasn't bad. But here indeed, are the best looking pair of cut-throats that I've ever seen in my life.

COCARDASSE: Sonofabitch!

PASSEPOIL: Be prudent!

NAVAILLE: The big one is superb. He's Don Quixote without Rosinante.

CHAVERNY: And the small one is Sancho Panza without his donkey. (Meanwhile, Cocardasse and Passepoil approach Gonzague who's chatting with Peyrolles and to this point hasn't noticed them.)

COCARDASSE & PASSEPOIL: (bowing very low) Milord!

GONZAGUE: (turning) Huh? What do these folks want? There

are no more kennels to rent.

COCARDASSE: (pointing proudly to Passepoil) This gentleman and I, we are old acquaintances of Milord, and we are coming to present our respects to him.

GONZAGUE: (low, to Peyrolles) They are not all dead?

PEYROLLES: Unfortunately, Lagardère has forgotten these two.

PASSEPOIL: If Milord is busy we are going to withdraw respectfully.

COCARDASSE: But we will return.

GONZAGUE: Ah, you know them, Peyrolles. Well, since they are your friends, take these brave lads to your office, let them drink and provide each of them new clothes a well provided purse, and let them wait my orders.

PASSEPOIL: (bowing) Milord, I had expected no less from your munificence.

COCARDASEE: And your memory. (bowing)

GONZAGUE: Go! (they bow)

PEYROLLES: (insolently) Follow me.

COCARDASSE: (raising his head) We are swordsmen and we will go ahead if you like. (they firmly plant their hats over their ears, raising their rapiers from the ragged corners of their cloaks and pass proudly before Peyrolles.)

CHAVERNY: (watching them leave) I find them a bit rough

with their friend. On what occasion was my dear cousin able to employ such wise guys? For it's not Peyrolles who knows them, it's him.

GONZAGUE: Gentlemen, you know why you've been convoked tonight, at eight o'clock at the Hotel Gonzague.

NAVAILLE: Yes, I believe it's a question of a family council.

GONZAGUE: Better than that, gentlemen, a solemn assembly of a tribunal wherein the Regent will be represented by the Vice-Chancellor d'Argenson.

CHAVERNY: Plague! Is it a question of the succession to the crown?

GONZAGUE: Marquis, we are speaking of serious things. You are going to have to prove your devotion to me, gentlemen.

NAVAILLE: We want to tell you our gratitude, Milord, for we are indebted to you.

GONZAGUE: Oh, Navaille, your land at Chamilles which was confiscated by royal decree is going to be returned to you. I have the promise of the Abbey Dubois.

NAVAILLE: It's still to you that I owe it.

GONZAGUE: I had you convoked, you Navaille, and you Chaneille in the character of relatives of Nevers. You Taranne and Albert as representatives of two Chatellux.

CHAVERNY: If it's not the Bourbon succession, it must be the Nevers succession under discussion.

GONZAGUE: Yes.

NAVAILLE: You can count on us.

THE OTHERS: Yes! Yes!

CHAVERNY: On me, too! Still, I want to know.

GONZAGUE: You are too curious, little cousin, it will ruin you.

CHAVERNY: But I am at least permitted to address a single question to you? What do I have to do?

GONZAGUE: Nothing, except join your voice to that of my friends.

CHAVERNY: (aside) Those voices have been purchased and mine is not for sale, by Jove.

(Knocking at the side door.)

NAVAILLE: They're knocking at that door.

GONZAGUE: You are mistaken. It cannot be she yet. Peyrolles is only supposed to bring her at seven o'clock.

CHAVERNY: No. (more knocking) Hold on. They're knocking again.

GONZAGUE: (aside) Then it is she.

NAVAILLE: Ought we to open?

GONZAGUE: No, gentlemen, I will await you this evening at the agreed moment, in the apartment of Princess Gonzague.

CHAVERNY: (aside) Oh! At all cost I will see Madame de

Gonzague before this assembly. (aloud) Come, Gentlemen, I think we are bothering my noble cousin now. To grave affairs this evening. But we will forget them tonight at the fest the Regent is giving to Mr. Law at the Palais Royal.

GONZAGUE: Till tonight, gentlemen.

ALL: Till tonight.

(Flor enters excitedly; she is richly dressed and covered with a veil which she raises at the sight of Gonzague; she is followed by a serving girl.)

FLOR: Ah, at last!

GONZAGUE: Why didn't you wait for Peyrolles?

FLOR: I thought your Peyrolles was forgetting me, and, as you had announced to me yesterday before Dame Angélique, my respectable Duenna, that Peyrolles was bringing me to your hotel, she really wanted, giving way to my entreaties, to replace your intendant, and she brought me here.

GONZAGUE: Dame Angélique, go prepare for Miss one of the apartments near mine; when everything's ready in that apartment, you will come find Miss.

(The Duenna leaves.)

FLOR: I shall no longer return to my prison?

GONZAGUE: No. This evening I will escort you to the ball being given by the Regent at the Palais Royal.

FLOR: At the Regent's Ball? Me, me, truly, really true? Ah, what will I wear? Will I ever be pretty enough?

GONZAGUE: At balls of the French Court, there's something which heightens and adorns even more than clothes.

FLOR: The smile?

GONZAGUE: No.

FLOR: Grace? Beauty?

GONZAGUE: You've got the smile, the grace, the beauty. The thing I will adorn you with is a name. And this name, unaware as you are of it, is an illustrious name, amongst the most illustrious names in France.

FLOR: Yes, Peyrolles also told me down there that he was taking me to a powerful family.

GONZAGUE: To a family related to our kings. Your father was a Duke.

FLOR: My father, in that case is dead. And my mother?

GONZAGUE: Your mother is a Princess.

FLOR: A Princess. And do you think she will love me?

GONZAGUE: I am sure of it.

FLOR: Oh, what joy. Well, it's singular—what you are telling me of my birth doesn't surprise me at all.

GONZAGUE: Truly?

FLOR: No. I've always dreamed that one day I would be a Duchess or a Queen. The name I am going to bear—will it be really nice, very sonorous?

GONZAGUE: First of all, I will tell you that your name as a child was never the one your bore down there.

FLOR: Ah, what was my name?

GONZAGUE: In your cradle you received the name of your mother. Your name is Blanche.

FLOR: Oh, that's strange.

GONZAGUE: Why this surprise?

FLOR: That reminds me.

GONZAGUE: Of what?

FLOR: Of a friend of mine, as good as she is beautiful.

GONZAGUE: You know a young girl named Blanche?

FLOR: Yes.

GONZAGUE: How old was she?

FLOR: My age. We were both children, and we loved each other tenderly. We were separated, but I've seen her again.

GONZAGUE: Ah! You've seen her again.

FLOR: Yes.

GONZAGUE: When? Where was it?

FLOR: First, about six months ago in Segovia. And then—

GONZAGUE: And then?

FLOR: What I'm telling you is interesting?

GONZAGUE: Everything that touches you interest me, my child. Look, this friend—this little Blanche—was she an orphan just like you?

FLOR: Yes, an orphan.

GONZAGUE: Spanish?

FLOR: No, French.

GONZAGUE: French! And who took care of her?

FLOR: An old woman.

GONZAGUE: Yes, but who paid the Duenna?

FLOR: A gentleman.

GONZAGUE: French, too?

FLOR: Yes, French.

GONZAGUE: (excitedly) And the name of this gentleman?

FLOR: (after a moment's hesitation) I've forgotten it. (aside) Lagardère is proscribed.

GONZAGUE: That's troubling. A French gentleman, established in Spain, can only be an exile. Unfortunately, there are a lot of them. You have no friends of your own age and I was already saying to myself: "I have some credit; I will get the gentleman who has the young girl pardoned, and my dear little Blanche will no longer be alone."

FLOR: Ah, you are nice. I've seen Blanche again in Paris.

GONZAGUE: Blanche is in Paris?

FLOR: Yes. I was arguing with the terrible Madame Angélique, who was preventing me from opening the curtains of the carriage. I at least wanted to glimpse the Palais Royal. At the corner of a small street the carriage grazed against some houses. I heard singing in a low room. I recognized the voice. I raised the curtain. Blanche was at the window. I let out a scream. I wanted to get out, but Madame Angélique was stronger than I and restrained me.

GONZAGUE: A street near the Palais Royal. Would you recognize that street?

FLOR: Sure. Besides, Madame Angélique told me it was the Rue Chantre. Why are you writing in your notebooks?

GONZAGUE: You must be able to see your friend again.

FLOR: Thanks.

DAME ANGÉLIQUE: (returning) Everything is ready, Miss.

GONZAGUE: Go, my child. Within an hour you'll see your mother.

FLOR: What will I say to her?

GONZAGUE: You must conceal nothing of the misfortunes of your past. Tell her the truth, the whole truth. Go, my child. The hour that is approaching will be the most solemn in your life.

FLOR: (leaving with Angélique) The little gypsy, daughter of a

Princess, cousin of the King of France. (she leaves)

GONZAGUE: Rue Chantre! Is she alone? Did he follow her? But is it really she? That's what must be determined, first of all. (rings—a valet appears) Have Mr. de Peyrolles come immediately. (the valet leaves). Why has this Lagardère waited so long? No, it can only be him. This young girl doesn't suspect, and nothing will disturb the comedy I've prepared. This little Flor will play her role admirably. Come on, Philippe, this is the great role of the dice. The millions in Law's bank, can, like the sequins in the *Thousand and One Nights*, change into dry leaves But the immense domains of Nevers will be of themselves alone a royal fortune. I want riches in default of happiness. At least, Madame de Gonzague ought to be grateful for the disinterested spouse who's going to return her daughter to her. How many kisses will she give to the little gypsy? (laughing) Believe then in the call of the blood, in the instinct of mothers (more somberly) then, in a short time, a young and beautiful princess can die of lassitude—so many young girls die of it—regrets, general mourning—inheritance finally secured and truly well earned.

PEYROLLES: (entering) Milord summoned me?

GONZAGUE: You told me that you suspect Lagardère of having put that poor Staupitz to death?

PEYROLLES: Yes, Milord.

GONZAGUE: Well, take care of yourself. I suspect Lagardère of being in Paris!

PEYROLLES: Mercy!

GONZAGUE: With Blanche de Nevers.

PEYROLLES: All will be lost.

GONZAGUE: They will arrive too late. And then I will be delighted to finish with that man. Put your spies in search. Have all the houses in the Rue Chantre searched.

PEYROLLES: Ah, it's there that—

GONZAGUE: Why are you trembling?

PEYROLLES: Milord is forgetting that on each of the men condemned and struck down by this Lagardère there was found words written in blood: "After the valet, the master."

GONZAGUE: Don't worry; I'll break this invincible sword.

PEYROLLES: With whom, sir?

GONZAGUE: With the Executioner.

CURTAIN

ACT II
SCENE 6

The dead speak.

The oratory of Princess Gonzague. Decorated in the rich and simple style of Louis XIV. A large window on the left. Doors in cutaway. That on the right leading outside, that on the left to the apartment of the Princess. To the right, near the audience, a prie-dieu. Above it a portrait of Philippe de Nevers. Near the audience, on the right and the left, curtains hiding hidden doors.

AT RISE, the room is empty, but soon the velour hanging on the left is gently raised, the head of the Hunchback appears. After assuring himself that no one is in the room, he slips in furtively, goes to the prie-dieu, bows to the image of Nevers, pulls from his pocket a book of hours and places it on the prie-dieu, and leaves mysteriously by the curtained door near the prie-dieu. After a moment, Madeleine and Chaverny enter from the opposite side.

MADELEINE: Wait here, Marquis. Madame consents to see you.

CHAVERNY: Finally!—You were saying, Dame Madeleine that my cousin is still sad?

MADELEINE: Ah, Marquis, she's like a dead person walking

in her tomb instead of sleeping in it. All day Madame stays on her knees on this prie-dieu, or seated in this large armchair—motionless, cold, and always alone. Soon it will be fifteen years that she hasn't left this apartment, the rest of them think her crazy, as for me, I remember, I know her misfortune. Her she is. Oh, sir, speak to her of the one she's always weeping for—and the one she no longer expects to see. (The Princess enters, severely dressed in mourning, walking slowly; she's still beautiful; in her pallor and sadness; with a gesture, or rather look she sends Madeleine away.)

PRINCESS: Mr. de Chaverny, to get to me, you invoked Nevers name. What do you want from me?

CHAVERNY: I must inform you, Madame, that soon, right here, at the request of Mr. de Gonzague, and by the express command of the Regent, a family tribunal has been convoked.

PRINCESS: I know it.

CHAVERNY: And you will appear before the tribunal?

PRINECESS: I will obey the Regent.

CHAVERNY: Madame, if I've guessed correctly, Mr. de Gonzague, has only one purpose in convoking this tribunal—to place himself in possession of the Nevers estate, placed in sequestration for fifteen years in the interest of the daughter of Philippe de Nevers, sole legitimate heir of his wealth.

PRINCESS: Mr. de Gonzague will furnish proof of the death of my daughter.

CHAVERNY: As for me, Madame, I am bringing you proof that your daughter exists.

PRINCESS: Proof, you said?

CHAVERNY: Here it is.

PRINCESS: Proof. (joyfully) At last!

CHAVERNY: I would have given you this letter sooner if I'd been allowed to get to you.

PRINCESS: (sadly) There's no signature on the letter.

CHAVERNY: The gentleman who wrote it is a brave and honest soldier.

PRINCESS: Why didn't he sign it?

CHAVERNY: The gentleman is exiled.

PRINCESS: You've been duped, as I have been twenty times, duped by tricksters and intriguers; when was this letter delivered to you?

CHAVERNY: Two months ago in Spain.

PRINCESS: And for the last two months nothing has come to prove the existence of my daughter, and once again, I repeat to you, Mr. Gonzague will himself bring proof of her death. But if the justice of men is for Mr. de Gonzague, I will have the justice of God on my side, until the hour in which he reveals herself to strike and punish. Leave me alone to pray and cry.

(She goes to pray on the prie-dieu. Chaverny bows deeply and leaves.)

PRINCESS: Haven't I suffered enough? How much longer will

this martyrdom last? If my daughter is with you, recall me; if my daughter is dead, my God—death, death!

(she bows her head and her glance is arrested by the Book of Hours that the Hunchback placed there.) This book of hours is not mine. Who put it here? My god, my God! This book, I recognize it. Yes, it's indeed the one I gave to Philippe, as I gave him our child. Lord, have you made a miracle? Ah, there's something in this book. Yes, a letter.... (reading)

"God will have pity if you will have faith. Your daughter exists and will be returned to you today." My daughter, my daughter exists! (reading) "More than ever beware of Gonzague, and remember the signal once agreed between you and Nevers." (speaking) His Motto—I am here. (reading) "During the assembly remain seated by the portrait of Nevers; when the time comes, for you, for you alone the dead will speak. Signed, Henri de Lagardère" (speaking) That handwriting is not unknown to me. Where have I seen it before? Ah, I remember. That writing is just like this (looking at the letter given her by Chaverny) Yes, the same hand penned these two letters—My God, then it's really true. Lord, if you've let me live, it's so you can return my daughter to me.

MADELEINE: (entering) Madame, the Vice-Chancellor, Mr. d'Argenson directed to preside over the family tribunal has come to ask you to come down to the large salon.

PRINCESS: No, no. I won't leave this room. (looking at the portrait)

MADELEINE: The Chancellor is at Madame's orders and will come to her if you will receive him here.

PRINCESS: Yes, here—here. (Madeleine leaves. She rereads the letter) "When the time comes, for you, you alone, the dead will speak" (she falls back into the chair near the curtained door) The dead will speak.

(Enter the family council, Gonzague, Chaverny, d'Argenson, Navaille, Peyrolles, valets in grand livery. They come through the large door on the left, bowing respectfully to the Princess. At a signal from Peyrolles the valets bring up seats, then, at another sign, the valets leave.)

GONZAGUE: Madame, these gentlemen are awaiting your good pleasure to take their seats.

PRINCESS: (so absorbed she saw no one enter, comes to herself) I cannot go to you, gentlemen. I thank you for being willing to come to me. (At a gesture from the Princess all take their seats.)

GONZAGUE: Will it please you, Madame to listen to the Vice-Chancellor.

PRINCESS: I am listening.

VICE CHANCELLOR: Madame, the Regent was counting on personally presiding at this assembly on account of the friendship he bears to Mr. de Gonzague, and the fraternal affection he used to have for the late Duke de Nevers. But administrative cases of the realm have retained His Highness at the palace. He has deigned to institute commissions and royal judges, Mr. de Villeroy de Lamoignon and myself. Mr. de Gonzague having exposed to us what he wants in fact and in law, we are ready to hear him.

GONZAGUE: First of all, let me be permitted to thank, all those who, on this occasion, have honored my family by their kindly solicitude, the Regent the first; I give thanks also to the Princess who, despite her languishing health and her love of solitude has willingly descended from the heights where she ordinarily dwells to this level of wretched human interests.

NAVAILLE: (low) Beautiful exordium.

GONZAGUE: Philippe de Loraine, Duke de Nevers was my cousin by blood, my brother by heart. Yes, we were truly brothers.

CHAVERNY: (aside) Brothers like Cain and Abel.

GONZAGUE: Fifteen years have unrolled and have not softened the bitterness of my sorrows. Philippe died the victim of revenge or betrayal. Unfortunately, the flight of the assassins did not allow justice to run its course. Gentlemen, I've reached the facts that have motivated this convocation—

CHAVERNY: (aside) we're going to hear some fine things, but if I must protest alone, I shall protest, praise God!

GONZAGUE: It was in marrying me that the Princess disclosed her secret but legitimate marriage with the late Duke of Nevers. At the same time, she affirmed the existence of a child born of that union. Written proofs were lacking. The child disappeared on the very night of her father's murder, and the Parlement of Paris issued a decree which suspends {within limits imposed by law} my rights to the inheritance of Nevers. That was to safeguard the interests of the young Blanche de Nevers; it was just, but the decree gave slander a fine weapon against me: a single obstacle it was said, separated me from an immense inheritance, and I was suspected of a crime; yes, a crime. (to the Princess) They told you, didn't they, Princess, that if you sought in vain for your daughter, if your efforts remained ineffective, it was because there was a mysterious hand in the shadows which distracted your investigations, led your pursuits in the wrong directions. They told you that?

PRINCESS: They told me that.

GONZAGUE They even told you that this mysterious hand was that of your husband.

PRINCESS: They told me that.

GONZAGUE: And you believed it?

PRINCESS: I believed it.

(murmurs)

GONZAGUE: Well, Madame, I answered all these infamous allegations by an ardent pursuit, more obstinate than yours. I, too, searched for the daughter of Nevers. I searched with my gold, with my heart, and today—

PRINCESS: Today, you are coming to tell me she is dead, right?

GONZAGUE: Today, I am coming tell you, you who scorn me, who hate me, that I, who respect you and love you—I am coming to you to say: Open your arms happy mother. I am going to put your child in them.

PRINCESS: (stunned) My child!

(general excitement)

CHAVERNY: Huh! I understand ill—

GONZAGUE: Your child that you have vainly sought, and that

I, with the aid of God have found.

CHAVERNY: By Jove! Now here's an ending I didn't expect. Let Miss Blanche de Nevers be brought here.

PRINCESS: (standing bolt upright) My daughter—my daughter is here, you say?

GONZAGUE: Yes.

PRINCESS: And it's you—you, who are returning her to me?

GONZAGUE: Here she is. (Flor is led in by Peyrolles) Miss de Nevers, go embrace your mother.

FLOR: My mother (she rushes to the Princess who remains motionless and cold.) (timidly) My mother—

PRINCESS: (to herself) He, Gonzague, returns my daughter to me?

NOVAILLLES (to Gonzague) This will forever confound slander and slanderers.

CHAVERNY: So much the better that my dear cousin has in his hands proof of Miss's birth?

GONZAGUE: Proof!

CHAVERNY: No doubt, the pages torn from the Chaplain's registry.

PRINCESS: Torn with my own hand, gentlemen, and delivered by me to Philippe in a fold sealed with three seals bearing the arms of his house.

GONZAGUE: You will learn by reading the declaration of Nathaniel, the Gypsy who found and raised the child how the fold disappeared.

PRINCESS: (to Flor) You don't have it.

FLOR: Me, I have nothing, Madame. I am only a poor girl raised by charity. They told me they were going to bring me to my mother. Oh, Madame, the poor little gypsy asks nothing of you, neither splendors nor riches; she only asks you to love her as she loves you.

GONZAGUE: Fine, very fine.

PRINCESS: My God! Inspire me, my God! This will be a horrible misfortune, this will be a crime that repudiates my child. My God! I implore you from the depths of my misery. (looking at the portrait and in a low voice) And you, you who ought to speak. Speak, I'm waiting.

HUNCHBACK: (behind the hanging) I'm here.

PRINCESS: (with joy) Ah! (aside) Prodigy! Prodigy!

GONZAGUE: Madame, you are forgetting if you wish ill to wish ill to the hand that places this treasure in yours. I only ask you to look at this poor child who is all trembling, all shattered by the greeting from her mother. (The Princess looks at Flor) See. Isn't she your daughter?

HUNCHBACK: (behind the hanging) No!

PRINCESS: (forcefully) No!

(murmurs)

CHAVERNY: (aside) By Jove, I ought to have said it. But how does she know?

GONZAGUE: This is too much, and human patience has its limits. Madame must have grave and very strong reasons to deny the evidence. You have such reasons?

HUNCHBACK: (still behind the hanging) Yes!

PRINCESS: Yes!

GONZAGUE: You will tell them to us today, in that case. Right now. It's necessary, isn't it, gentlemen. It's necessary.

ALL: Yes, yes.

CHAVERNY: (aside) Poor cousin. The devil is caught in his own spider net.

GONZAGUE: Ah, the Nevers fortune is a fine prize; some impostor, speculating on your tenderness, has announced to you that he's found, saved your daughter?

CHAVERNY: He enrages to give pleasure.

GONZAGUE: They told you, didn't they, that she was alive? (silence. Enraged.) Why, answer—

D'ARGENSON: Answer, Madame!

HUNCHBACK: Living.

PRINCESS: (forcefully) Living—despite you and through the protection of God!

GONZAGUE: Gentlemen, I blush to reply with a single word.

Decide if you please, between the Princess and me.

D'ARGENSON: Since Madame de Gonzague knows where she believes her daughter is—let her present her! Written evidence, and invoked by the Princess. Those pages torn from the registry of the chapel de Caylus ought to be produced— In the name of the King, we will adjourn the Council for three days.

PRINCESS: I accept. I will have my daughter, and I will have the proof.

HUNCHBACK: This evening.

PRINCESS: (low) This evening?

HUNCHBACK: At the Regent's Ball.

GONZAGUE: (to Flor) Poor child. Now God alone can render you the heart of your mother.

(Peyrolles comes to take her)

FLOR: (going to the Princess) Madame, I don't know God's secrets, but whether you be my mother or not, I respect you and I love you. (she kneels)

PRINCESS: (raising her with kindness) You are not an accomplice, I see that. I don't wish you ill for it, child, go. (Peyrolles leads Flor away. The Princess rings and Madeleine appears.) Madeleine have my litter prepared for this evening.

GONZAGUE: A litter for you, Madame, you, who for the last fifteen years haven't left this apartment?

PRINCESS: (to Madeleine) Bring my jewel box, too.

GONZAGUE: Your diamonds! Where are you going tonight, Madame?

PRINCESS: To the Regent's Ball.

GONZAGUE: You! You?

PRINCESS: Me. As of today, my mourning is over! I've found my daughter! Till tonight., gentlemen, till tonight .

(While Chaverny and the others surround and bow to the Princess, Gonzague holds himself apart, and from behind him, the Hunchback slips in and appears so that only Gonzague can see and hear him.)

GONZAGUE: (to himself) Who is it who's done all this?

HUNCHBACK: (low) Who? The one you've never known how to find or catch.

GONZAGUE: (low) Lagardère!

HUNCHBACK: (low) Yes, Lagardère—who I cam deliver to you.

GONZAGUE: You?

HUNCHBACK: Yes.

GOZAGUE: Where's that?

HUNCHBACK: At the Regent's Ball if you get me invited.

(Gonzague looks at the Hunchback with amazement as he bows and slips back behind the tapestry, as the others, having been dismissed, prepare to leave.)

CURTAIN

ACT III
SCENE 7

Cocardasse and Passepoil.

A low hall in the house on the Rue Chantre. Door at the back covered with shutters opening on a window giving on the street. Door on the right, mid-stage, opening on a stairway whose lower steps can be seen leading to Blanche's room. To the left, a stairway leading to Lagardère's room above.

AT RISE, Blanche is seated at a small table lit by a lamp. She writes. Tonio is setting the table.

TONIO: (to himself) Truly, since we've been in Paris I'm all alone to do the work. (to Blanche) Señora, old Maritana, your respectable Duenna is not coming down to help me set the table?

BLANCHE: The poor woman is really very ill, and I am forced to put her to bed. (pause) Tonio?

TONIO: Señora?

BLANCHE: Has my friend returned yet?

TONIO: I hear steps above in his room. He's still locked in with the Hunchback, that I saw just now on the small stairway which gives on the alley, and permits him to come to the master without ever passing through here.

BLANCHE: Who can this man be who so carefully avoids our sight?

TONIO: That's it! Who can he be? And is it not quite extraordinary to see a man like the master frequent closely a bandy-legged person twisted like a corkscrew? This Hunchback comes and goes as if the house were his own. He's almost always upstairs. Yet the boss won't allow himself to be seen with him. They are never seen together in the street. This greatly intrigues the neighbors, and wait, not later than just now, an old gentleman, of very venerable mien came to ask me a bunch of questions.

BLANCHE: What did he ask you?

TONIO: He asked me who we were, what we were doing, where we came from, your age, that of the master. If you were his wife or his daughter? At what time he left, at what time he returned.

BLANCHE: You didn't reply, Tonio?

TONIO: No, no, nothing. (aside) At first, but the old questioner was so generous and then he told me he was warden of our parish, and if one has no trust in a Church warden—(aloud) He's very late. The master isn't coming down. I really want you to sup early. I would be able to enter the crowd at the Regent's Ball. It seems it will be superb. There'll be more than a hundred thousand lamps. Suppose I go call the master?

BLANCHE: Respect the secret or the response of my friend. Go up to Maritana and make sure she doesn't need anything.

TONIO: (aside) That's the thing. All I lack is to be a sick person's attendant. (he goes out)

BLANCHE: (resuming her writing) Mother, he told me that God has preserved for me the treasure of your tenderness. He told me that one day through him you would be restored to me—for a long time I saw you in all my dreams; you are in all my prayers. It seems to me you must know all I am thinking. And when you read these pages written during my hours of solitude you will know my heart which has not kept one secret from you, mother. I am more alone here than in Segovia. My friend is almost always out. Perhaps he's seeking you. But why, when he's reaching the final goal of his life is he more sad and more silent? Oh, you will love him, won't you, mother? you will love him because—(Lagardère quietly descends the stairs and without being heard arrives behind her. Lagardère is wearing a simple and severe gentleman's suit. She continues without seeing him.)—he has given his life for me, he saved me! Without him, where would I be? A bit of dust in a poor, small tomb. And what mother, were she a duchess or a cousin of a king, would not be proud to have the Chevalier Henri de Lagardère as a son. The proudest, the bravest, the most generous of men. Whatever may be the name that birth has given him, Lagardère will be worthy of that name. Oh, I would have all the joys of heaven! Till tomorrow, my beloved mother, till tomorrow.

LAGARDÈRE: (softly and sadly) No, Blanche, not till tomorrow, till tonight. For tonight you will embrace your mother.

BLANCHE: (with joy) Tonight!

LAGARDÈRE: I saw her just now. She has kept as sacred in her soul the memory of your father. She will love you as she loved him: you will be happy, child. But you must tear up what you've written You must never speak of me to your mother. You must forget me once you are in her arms.

BLANCHE: Forget you, you, Henri!

LAGARDÈRE: Yes, as I will forget a mad dream. Your mother is a great lady, a very great lady. As for me, I am only a poor gentleman. And what's my name? It comes to me from ruined walls in which I sheltered my rights as an orphan child. God is my witness that I have never had any other thought than to return to her mother the sacred deposit confided to me by the father.

BLANCHE: Henri!—In that case you no longer love me?

LAGARDÈRE: Ah!, Blanche, nothing can separate me from my courage or my reason. We were building on sand. A breath sufficed to overturn the frail edifice of my hope. When I left Spain after so many dangers and struggles, it seemed to me that on seeing you your mother would open her arms to me and clasp me, all dusty from traveling, to her heart intoxicated with joy. I was happy—no, I was mad. The closer the time comes, the greater the distance that separates us. A mother wants to be and must be obeyed. Your mother, rightfully proud of her race and of her name will order you to forget me—and you will forget me.

BLANCHE: No, no! Have you calculated the distance to protect me, to defend me? Would I love my mother less if she were poor? No! I will ask only her tenderness. And if she makes me pay the price of my love for it—Oh, Henri, Henri…

LAGARDÈRE: You will obey.

BLANCHE: No. I will die.

LAGARDÈRE: Blanche, you've just paid me for all that I've

done for you. You owe me nothing more, child. You wouldn't want your mother to suspect for a moment that the one you've thought worthy of your love, so chaste and so pure—you wouldn't want her to say of Lagardère: "This man made a profession of his devotion! My daughter is the richest heiress in France and he's not returning her to me, he's selling her to me."—Oh, you won't do that, Blanche. You won't do that.

(rapping at the door)

TONIO: (returning) They're rapping, I believe.

LAGARDÈRE: Yes, open. (looking at the clock hanging on the wall) Here's the time that has to come. (Tonio admits a woman bearing two packages) Place what you are bringing there. (The woman places her packages on the table near Blanche and leaves at a sign from Lagardère. Tonio follows her to the door.)

TONIO: (in the door way. Oh, there they are—lighting the street lamps. Oh, God—if they had supped. (remains in the doorway.)

LAGARDÈRE: Blanche—open the packages.

BLANCHE: (opening) A fancy dress.

LAGARDÈRE Quite simple. But poor Lagardère will be able to give you a more precious jewel, for you than the most beautiful diamond in the crown of France. This jewel, this treasure—here it is, my child. (he presents her the folded sealed fold that he pulls from his breast) Here in this fold under triple seal are the proofs of your birth. Incontestable proofs that you are going to deliver right now to your mother in the presence of Milord, the Regent.

BLANCHE: Oh, Henri, it will be you who gives them to him.

LAGARDÈRE: Me? Do I even know if I will be allowed to appear at your side? I told you, I'm exiled. And to enter the Palace of the Regent I would need a safe-conduct signed by the Regent himself.

COCARDASSE: (pushing Tonio aside who tries to prevent his entering) Ah, damn it all! Must I forever find you blocking my path? Is this indeed No. 7, Rue de Chantre?

LAGARDÈRE: Yes, and it is really I who gave you the rendez-vous here, Master Cocardasse. Now take these packages and put them up in Blanche's room. (Tonio leaves, to Blanche) Although ill, the good Maritana will help you to dress. This is the hour that your mother is expecting you. If at this hour I haven't come, this man will replace me. He will take you to the Palais Royal, escorting the chair porters who will be here at midnight. Don't forget to bring the sealed fold. All your future, all your happiness is in there!

BLANCHE: My happiness! (she leaves)

LAGARDÈRE: You heard what I want of you?

COCARDASSE: Perfectly. If there's nothing else to do, I alone will suffer and will miss my little apprentice less. The scamp left me sleeping in the office to run after a scullery wench, ugly as the seven deadly sins. But this Vesuvius of a Passepoil takes fire like oakum. I was dozing under the chimney when I heard these words fall on my ear. "At ten o'clock, Rue de Chantre, no 7. Lagardère." At that name I leapt from my chair, and I saw nothing but the silhouette of a little hunchback vanishing like a shadow in the gangway.

LAGARDÈRE: You are on time—

COCARDASSE: To come to my little Parisian when he calls me, I would pass through fire. We said that I would come at midnight and that I would escort the little one—to?

LAGARDÈRE: To the Palais Royal, at the circle of Diana under the great Indian tent. There's where the Regent will be hanging out. That's where I will be. If I am unable to return here have I not calculated everything, foreseen everything? No, Listen if some unforeseen obstacle prevents the execution of the order I've given you, come warn me.

COCARDASSE: I understand. I will go to the Palais Royal.

LAGARDÈRE: And, as soon as you see me you will show me your naked hand. If some misfortune has occurred, a danger to Blanche, let your glove fall.

COCARDASSE: Don't worry. For something bad to happen to the child on the way, the Devil would have to be in it, for she will be well protected, praise God!

LAGARDÈRE: I know it.

TONIO: (coming in) Maritana is dressing the Señora.

LAGARDÈRE: Tonio, you will let this gentleman enter when he comes to escort Miss to the Regent's Ball. Master Cocardasse, till midnight.

COCARDASSE: Till midnight.

(Cocardasse leave; Lagardère goes up the stairway to his rooms.)

TONIO: The Master's going to dress, too. Everybody will go amuse themselves, except me. I will remain here to protect Maritana. (looking) Oh, as to that, no! I will have my share of the festivity. (looking) Oh, God, how it's shining there. Oh, not to be able to do as the others! (turning) And the Señora will take more than an hour to dress. Suppose I set the clock ahead to hurry her. That's an idea! (standing on a chair he sets the clock ahead). There. Once the masters have gone I will let Maritona snooze and I will head for the Palais Royal. Huh! It seems to me someone's coming down the stairway which gives on the alley. Could it be the Master has left? (looking out) No, it's the Hunchback sliding along the length of the house. Ah, that one isn't going to the ball.

(At this moment a woman enveloped in a cloak slips quickly into the house. It's Flor, very upset)

FLOR: Ah, I've found my way again. I recognized the house, yes, she must be here.

TONIO: Huh! Who's coming into our house like this?

FLOR: (raising her cloak) It's me, Tonio.

TONIO: Ah, the gypsy! The little pagan made a fortune.

FLOR: I want to see Blanche, and see her right away.

TONIO: Let you see the Señora! That's still forbidden here, as there.

FLOR: Oh, I will see her. I will speak to her, despite you. Despite the whole world.

BLANCHE (entering, wearing a red-domino) Flor! You here!

FLOR: (low to Blanche) Lagardère is with you, right?

BLANCHE: Yes.

FLOR: Oh, God be praised. I've arrived in time. (low) I'm coming to save the two of you.

BLANCHE: You!

FLOR: Call him, let him come immediately.

BLANCHE: Tonio, my friend is in his room. Beg him to come down.

FLOR: Ouf! I cannot breathe! I ran so much. I was so afraid of being noticed, followed. So no one would suspect my departure from the house in the Rue Saint Maggiore, I locked myself in my room, and I leapt through the window into the garden.

BLANCHE: Ah!

FLOR: A little mezzanine—it was nothing. I would have jumped from a third floor if necessary.

BLANCHE: My God! Why? (Tonio comes down) Well?

TONIO: No one's there. The Master has gone out.

FLOR: Gone! Why in that case he's ruined.

BLACHE: Ruined—him?

FLOR: Hush! Send the boy to watch outside and to run warn us if he sees anyone heading toward this house.

BLANCHE: You heard, Tonio!

TONIO: Yes, Señora. I am going to watch outside. (aside) At least to the end of the street to see the illumination from the palace. (leaves closing the door behind him)

BLANCHE: Now we are alone, speak, speak! What new danger threatens us?

FLOR: You were right, Blanche, when you told me that you had a terrible enemy. Implacable. That enemy, I know him now, and it's through me, through me, you understand, through me that he has learned of your presence in Paris. Oh, I am sure of it, it's you that he's pursuing and wants to ruin. You have to go to the Regent's Ball tonight, right?

BLANCHE: Yes.

FLOR: And the Chevalier Lagardère announced to you that you would find, that you would embrace your mother there?

BLANCHE: Yes.

FLOR: Your mother to whom you must deliver a sealed slip of paper containing proof of your birth?

BLANCHE: Yes. How do you know all that?

FLOR: I know a lot of things. I know what you yourself are possibly unaware of. I know your name is Blanche de Nevers, that you are the daughter of the Duke of Lorraine, and the heiress to an immense fortune. A fortune that would have belonged to your enemy if he had been able to make you disappear. Despairing, no question, of finding you, the wretch still wants to steal your name, your wealth, and your mother's tenderness. He was not afraid to present in your place, a poor girl without knowledge that he was committing a crime; but heaven permitted this involuntary accomplice to overhear the new plot being hatched against you. She learned just now that to assure the success of this infamy, they do not recoil before abduction and murder. She's coming to tell you they intend to use me to ruin you. But at the risk of my life I will save you. Yes, Blanche I will save you.

BLANCHE: What! It was you?

FLOR: It was me they intended to use. And one moment I played in good faith an infamous role. Blanche, moments are precious. Lagardère is not here. But you are going to have protection greater than his. Come, Blanche, let's get out of here. I am going to take you to your mother. She will know very well how to defend her child.

BLANCHE: No, no! I won't leave this house to which Lagardère is going to come—where some trap is going to be laid. I will save him or I will be ruined with him. I'm staying. I want to wait for him.

FLOR: Wait for him? Will that give you time to get there? Have you got the letter, the sealed parchment? You mustn't let yourself be separated from it.

BLANCHE: It's there, in my room, on my make up table.

FLOR: I am going to find it, because, as soon as Lagardère arrives we will leave, Blanche, we will leave. And if he's too late, you will let me do what he would have done. (going up the stairs)

BLANCHE: Forgive me, mother, but I won't be a cowardly ingrate. (listening) They're walking in the street. They're stopping before this door. There are several persons there—Tonio, didn't warn me—Perhaps through this window I'll be able to distinguish—(looking) Yes, a litter with porters. (Midnight sounds on the clock) And there's the hour that Henri should return.

(she opens the door. As soon as she does so a heavy veil is thrown over her head by Passepoil who chokes off her scream)

PASSEPOIL: There she is caught. Oh! (Blanche tries to get free of the hand Passepoil has placed over her mouth.) Oh, pretty little hand. It scratched me, but it's pretty.

PEYROLLES: (entering) Quickly, put her in the chair I brought. Ah, wait.

FLOR: (returning) I've got the parchment.

(Peyrolles quickly seizes the parchment and stifles her screams.)

CURTAIN

ACT III
SCENE 8

A party at the Palais Royal.

A richly hung tent, opening at the back on the garden of the Palais Royal through large velour draperies that are lowered when the act begins. Side entrances. Under the tent, tables, seats, rich candelabras. The total effect is bizarre. The candelabras are palm trees in gold and the candles burn in exotically shaped crystals. In any event, the décor is composed to be in harmony with the great decoration of the fest which is revealed when the draperies at the back are raised.

NAVAILLE Word of honor, we're in a fairy palace.

CHAVERNY: (to Breant who is straightening things up) Hey! Here's Master Breant the respected servant of the Usher of His Royal Highness. He's going to tell us if this tent is the one reserved for the Regent.

BREANT: Yes, sir. (pointing) It communicates from this side with his apartments. That's the way His Royal Highness will come; it's here he will rest from the weariness of the festivities.

NAVAILLE: Splendid festivity. I no longer recognize the garden.

CHAVERNY: Oh, we are no longer at the Palais Royal, rue Saint Honoré. We are in Louisiana on the shores of the Mississippi; Mr. Law wanted to show the shareholders the beautiful country where this river of gold flows.

NAVAILLE: We've been assured that this tent is a faithful copy of a savage wigwam.

CHAVERNY: A wigwam in Nacaret velours—with gold tassels. Savages lodge well.

NAVAILLE Look—

CHAVERNY: Yes, yes, these Indian trophies, are also most pure Mohican. Bows, arrows, clubs in gold. Everything's made of gold in the Mississippi. The river itself rolls in waves of gold.

NAVAILLE: (after peeking through the curtain at back) Oh, decidedly they intend that nothing be lacking in local color. Here's a company of French guards who've just occupied their posts. And all these brave soldiers are disguised as Indians.

CHAVERNY: Really! Let's go see that, gentlemen, let's go see that. (They leave by the back. Breant reenters followed by the Hunchback dressed agreeably in black, with lace frills and ruffles, etc.

BREANT: What! Hop o' my thumb. It's you who wrote to the Regent this letter he's re-read three times?

HUNCHBACK: It was myself.

BREANT: He's going to give an audience to you.

HUNCHBACK: It's very possible.

BREANT: To a hunchback!

HUNCHBACK: Oh, my wit's better than my figure. First of all, I know how to show gratitude for little services done me. If you will escort me immediately to His Highness this double crown is yours. (giving it to him)

BREANT: Here comes His Highness. Take back your double crown, little man, I haven't earned it.

HUNCHBACK: Keep it all the same, with this one.

BREANT: So, it's like everything here. Your hump is made of gold.

HUNCHBACK: That's quite possible.

REGENT: (enters chatting with d'Argenson) What you say surprises me greatly.

CHANCELLOR: I've given Your Royal Highness a faithful report of what took place at the Hotel Gonzague. A mother who refuses to embrace the child she wept over for fifteen years, and that was presented to her. An inconsolable Artemis who is coming to a fest like this. It's all quite strange, and I am beginning to fear for Madame Gonzague's reason. Finally, I will see her tonight. (turning) Who is there?

BREANT: A man to whom Your Royal Highness wanted to give an audience.

REGENT: Me? Who did I promise an audience to here, this evening?

HUNCHBACK: (bowing) To the Chevalier de Lagardère, Milord.

REGENT: That's true. Later, d'Argenson, later. (D'Argenson leaves)

REGENT: Approach. It's you who wrote me?

HUNCHBACK: No, Milord.

REGENT: (smiling) Indeed, you cannot be Lagardère.

HUNCHBACK: I was never able to be a Light-Cavalryman.

REGENT: What's your name?

HUNCHBACK: Folks like me have no other name than the nickname they are given.

REGENT: Where are you living?

HUNCHBACK: In the Hotel of Prince de Gonzague.

REGENT: In the Hotel de Gonzague—you?

HUNCHBACK: And the rents are so expensive.

REGENT: This Lagardère used to be a determined bravo. What does he hope from me?

HUNCHBACK: He's done his best to expiate his follies.

REGENT: What are you to him? If I want to see him, where will I find him?

HUNCHBACK: I cannot answer that question, Milord.

REGENT: I know all I want to know. (The Hunchback is quiet)

HUNCHBACK: Lagardère is protected from all investigations, and the action that he is going to take to acquit his conscience—he won't renew it.

REGENT: He's doing it from regret?

HUNCHBACK: From regret.

REGENT: Why?

HUNCHBACK: Because all the happiness of his life is staked on this role he will be unable to play.

REGENT: And who is forcing him to do what he is doing?

HUNCHBACK: An oath.

REGENT: Made to whom?

HUNCHBACK: To a man who was going to die.

REGENT: And that man's name?

HUNCHBACK: That man's name was Philippe de Lorraine, Duke de Nevers.

REGENT: (sitting down) Yes, he wrote me that—my poor Philippe, I really loved him. Since they killed him on me, I don't know if I've shaken the hand of a sincere friend. (aloud) Why has Mr. de Lagardère delayed so long in addressing himself to me?

HUNCHBACK: Because he wanted Miss de Nevers to be of an age to know her friends and her enemies.

REGENT: Then it wasn't Miss de Nevers that Gonzague brought today to her mother?

HUNCHBACK: No, Milord.

REGENT: Mr. de Gonzague was deceived?

HUNCHBACK: No, Milord.

REGENT: You are daring to say—?

HUNCHBACK: It's not me speaking, it's Mr. de Lagardère. As for me, I know nothing.

REGENT: And Mr. de Lagardère has proof of what he's maintaining?

HUNCHBACK: Yes, Milord.

REGENT: Even that which most needs confirmation—he pretends to know the murderer. He writes me that he was in the moats of Caylus at the moment of the murder.

HUNCHBACK: He was there.

REGENT: And the assassin is still living?

HUNCHBACK: Your Royal Highness shall have only to say the word and Mr, de Lagardère will point him out to you tonight.

REGENT: Then this Lagardère is in Paris? If he's in Paris he's mine. (grabs a bell and rings it.)

HUNCHBACK: (pulling out his watch) Milord, Mr. de Lagardère is waiting for me outside Paris—on a road that I will not disclose to you were you to put me to the Question. Ten o'clock has struck. And if Mr. Lagardère receives no information from me before eleven his horse will be galloping toward the frontier. He has relays and your police will be able to do nothing.

REGENT: You will be hostage.

HUNCHBACK: Oh, for the time Your Highness insists on keeping me, I am completely at your orders.

REGENT: (to Secretary who enters and bows, waiting for an order) I beg you, bring me a safe conduct, signed in blank and under seal, and countersigned in blank. (The Secretary bows and leaves.) This Chevalier de Lagardère treats me as one power to another. He's sending me an ambassador.

HUNCHBACK: A very humble one, Milord.

REGENT: How much time will he need to get here?

HUNCHBACK: Two hours.

REGENT: That's for the best. It will serve as an intermission between the ballet and the supper.

(The Secretary returns with the safe-conduct.)

REGENT: (signing) Mr. de Lagardère has not committed unpardonable sins— Here's the safe-conduct. Inform Mr. de Lagardère that any violence on his part will break the effect of this parchment.

HUNCHBACK: The time for violence has passed. Mr. de Lagardère has only one blow left to strike. He told these murderers: "You will all die by my hand." There were eight of them. The Chevalier has met six of them and they are dead.

REGENT: By his hand? (The Hunchback bows) And the others?

HUNCHBACK: This is what Mr. de Lagardère has directed me to tell Your Royal Highness. The seventh murderer is only a valet. Don't count him. The eighth is the master. This one has to die. If Your Highness doesn't want the Executioner to punish him, let the guilty be given a sword and Mr. de Lagardère will do justice.

REGENT: (giving him the parchment) In two hours!

HUNCHBACK: (bowing) In two hours.

REGENT: Here!

HUNCHBACK: Here!

REGENT: That's fine.

(The Regent leaves followed by the Secretary)

BREANT: (entering) Well, my good man, did you get what you needed?

HUNCHBACK: Yes. Now, I want to see the party.

BREANT: Fine dancer you will make.

HUNCHBACK: I brought a much more gallant outfit than this. You will allow me to dress in your place?

BREANT: I owe you something for your two crowns.

HUNCHBACK: And here are four more. I always pay in advance.

BREANT: His hump hemorrhages gold crowns.

CHAVERNY: (entering with others) Holá! Master Breant! (he points to the Hunchback who walks amongst them looking at them with his lorgnette) What the devil of a creature is that? Eh, why one would say, eh, yes, he's the ten thousand crown man. The man of the kennel, Aesop.

NAVAILLE: (entering) Gentlemen, something extraordinary is going to take place.

ALL: Bah!

NAVAILLE: Mr. de Bonnivet, the Captain of the Guards has just doubled all posts and two new companies of French Guards have just arrived in the Court. What's it all mean?

CHAVERNY: Ask the sorcerer.

HUNCHBACK: Sorcerer. Perhaps you don't know how well you have spoken.

CHAVERNY: Suspect the Devil in person. Inform us what it's all about.

HUNCHBACK: Do you believe in ghosts, sir?

ALL: In ghosts!

CHAVERNY: You've become morbid, Aesop.

HUNCHBACK: When the hour of justice strikes, and it always strikes, whether sooner or later, a man, a messenger from the tomb, a ghost emerges from the ground—because God wills it. That man sometimes accomplishes his fatal mission despite himself. If he's strong, he strikes, if he's weak, he slides, he crawls, he goes on until he reaches the level of the ear of the powerful, and, at the appointed hour, the astonished avenger hears the name of the murderer.

NAVAILLE: What murderer does he mean? Do we know him?

CHAVERNY: Tell us his name.

ALL: Yes, his name.

HUNCHBACK: His name would shock you if I told you. But on the first step of the throne the Regent is seated, and soon a voice will cry out to him, "Highness, the murderer is in the gilded crowd. Yesterday, perhaps, your royal hand shook his bloody hand." And the avenger has risen up saying, "By the living God, justice will be done."

CHAVERNY: Could there be an assassin here?

NAVAILLE: The man is mad.

HUNCHBACK: (turning back on his path) There! There! Take it easy, the guilty man is not hereabouts. Don't pull such sad faces, we are at a fest. Laugh, gentlemen, laugh. My ghost is in a good mood. And if he knows everything, this devil of a ghost, the things of the present as well as the past, he came to the fest; he's waiting for His Royal Highness to point his finger at him, clever hands after bloody hands, clever gentlemen who make the cup jump at this vast bridge table where Mr. Law has the honor of being banker.

NAVAILLE: Will you shut up?

CHAVERNY: Do you take yourself to be the one he's talking about? Wretched abortion, you are going to declare immediately that your words have no application to me. If not, I—

HUNCHBACK: If not—you will kill poor Aesop in single combat. Come on. You will make better use, I am sure of it, of the good blade given you by Henríquez, the armorer of Segovia.

CHAVERNY: How do you know that?

NAVAILLE: Should we call our valets to drive this wise-acre out of here?

HUNCHBACK: For God's sake! Don't get angry. Tomorrow you will all need the hunchback. Tomorrow you will pay good cash in crowns on his back to make a desk. But until tomorrow let me amuse myself, let me laugh about the inventions of false news, of dodgers from on high, and jugglers from way down below. Let me laugh at frustrated ambitions, and envenomed grudges, at great politicians in retreat whose pride or egotism cannot accustom itself to silence and being forgotten. Let me also laugh at the uneasy intriguers who want to revive the Fronde And overturn France if need be to regain lost positions or regretted honors. Let me laugh, gentlemen, let me laugh. (he leaves, laughing)

CHAVERNY: He's a real sorcerer—is that hunchback.

GONZAGUE: (entering) Of what hunchback are you speaking, gentlemen?

CHAVERNY: Your tenant. Can you believe that he is at the Regent's Ball tonight?

GONZAGUE: It was I who gave him a card to enter.

ALL: You—

GONZAGUE: (aside) We'll see if he keeps the promise he made me.

NAVAILLE Gentlemen, I'm beginning to be uneasy The Lieutenant of Police must be on the track of some conspiracy.

CHAVERNY: Really? Ands why?

NAVAILLE: Mr. Bonnivet, the Captain of the Guards has just given the order to let everyone in but not to let anyone out.

GONZAGUE: (aside) That's what it is. Lagardère has been announced, expected. (aloud) You haven't seen my Intendant, Mr. Peyrolles in the crowd?

NAVAILLE No. But I am going to announce Milord the Regent with the Princess Gonzague.

(Enter the Regent, the Princess, and guards.)

REGENT: Lean on my arm, Madame. After such a profound retreat, the uproar of this crowd, the dazzle of these lights must weigh on you and disturb you a little—

PRINCESS: Ah, Milord. I feel that I am no longer of this world, and if, for once, I have consented to return to it—

REGENT: It's because you are expecting someone in the name of Nevers who has promised you to come.

PRINCESS: Yes.

REGENT: I, too, am expecting Mr. Lagardère.

PRINCESS: Lagardère!

GONZAGUE: What can they be talking about?

REGENT: Isn't he the one you are hoping to see?

PRINCESS: It's he. He's the one who promised to return my daughter to me.

REGENT: (low) He accuses your husband of an odious crime and base intrigue. Oh, misfortune to this Lagardère if he's merely a slanderer.

PRINCESS: He will have proof.

REGENT: Allow me to still doubt that.

GONZAGUE: Always proud, always implacable. But I will have my revenge.

AN USHER: (announcing) Mr. Law, Director of the Indian Companies.

(The Regent takes a few steps toward the Ambassador and Mr. Law who bow deeply)

REGENT: The hero of the fest. The fest is going to begin.

(On a signal from the Regent the tent flaps are raised revealing the gardens transformed into a Louisiana landscape. Trees surrounded by creepers. Blue mountains, prairies, and the golden stream of the Mississippi unfold in waves of gold on the lawn. Groups of young Indians, girls and warriors, smoking the peace pipe. All the Indians are richly dressed. The Regent and the Princess, the Ambassador, Mr. Law and the ladies of the court mount a platform with chairs and takes seats. Large velour covered benches are provided for the courtiers.)

BONNIVET: This way, gentlemen, this way.

REGENT: Why, this commotion, this uproar? Answer, Mr. Captain of the Guards.

BONNIVET: Milord, a gentleman wanted to force the password and leave the palace.

REGENT: You must arrest this gentleman if he doesn't respect an order I have given.

BONNIVET: This gentleman is a terrible adversary, Milord. He knocked over, wounded those of my guards who blocked him; he dared to cross swords with me, but at the name of Your Royal Highness he put his sword in his scabbard.

REGENT: And who is this gentleman?

BONNIVET: No one knows him.

REGENT: And where is he?

BONNIVET: He lost himself in the crowd where my guards are searching for him now.

GONZAGUE: (aside) That must be Lagardère.

REGENT: Find that man, sir. Seize him, and bring him here. I insist on it.

LAGARDÈRE: (dressed elegantly, but severely as a gentleman, has entered and heard) I am respectfully at the orders of Your Royal Highness.

REGENT: You will give us an account for your conduct, sir. And first of all, you will tell us your name.

LAGARDÈRE: Henri, Chevalier de Lagardère.

GONZAGUE, THE REGENT, & THE PRINCESS: Lagardère!

CHAVERNY: My gentleman armorer! The exile was Lagardère.

REGENT: (severely) Sir, it's by our good pleasure, we recognize it, that you are here. But we did not provide in our agreement that that you come to disturb our festivities, and draw your sword against officers of our house. That makes us too soon repent our clemency in your regard.

LAGARDÈRE: Milord, I wanted to leave the palace; it was an important matter that called me outside. To respond to that call I didn't hesitate to risk my life. But I didn't wish to incur Your Royal Highness's disgrace.

PRINCESS: (low) Ah, Milord, you know what this man promised to do.

REGENT: I have great need to remind myself of it, Madame. (aloud) Mr. D'Argenson will you reassemble the persons who compose the family tribunal that you were presiding over in our name. (To Bonnivet) Captain, a word, I beg you.

(As those who are not of the Council are about to leave, Lagardère approaches Gonzague.)

LAGARDÈRE: (in a low voice) The night of September 12th I told you, "If you do not come to Lagardère, Lagardère will come to you." You haven't come to me, and here I am. (going to the Princess to whom he bows deeply) Here, as in the moats of Caylus, as in the oratorio of Gonzague, I am completely devoted to Your Highness.

GONZAGUE: (aside) The hunchback kept his word. He's delivering my enemy to me—But what the devil is Peyrolles doing?

PRINCESS: And my daughter, sir—where is my daughter?

LAGARDÈRE: I was going to seek her, but someone other than myself is going to bring her here.

PEYROLLES (slipping in unnoticed and going to Gonzague) Milord.

GONZAGUE: Ah!. At last. The young girl and the parchment?

PEYROLLES: We got them. At the little house in the Rue Saint Maggiore.

GONZAGUE: Fine. (aside) Now, for the two of us, Lagardère. And I will show you neither grace nor mercy. (in a loud voice, abruptly) I humbly beg Your Royal Highness not to send anyone away. If a man like Mr. Lagardère has need of shadows and mystery, a man like myself, Milord, only needs light and brightness. Mr. de Lagardère, I know, is coming to accuse me, and I would like this strange accusation to have even more witnesses. It's not merely before you, Milord, or you Madame, that I intend to confound him, to crush the slander before all.

REGENT: I approve of you, Mr. de Gonzague, if the attack has been dull and secret, publicity and clarity will be the defense. (to the other lords) Stay, Gentlemen.

GONZAGUE: Oh, I won't have to defend myself, Milord. I

don't see anyone with Mr. de Lagardère who pretends to be the daughter of Philippe de Lorraine.

LAGARDÈRE: Milord, I had to assure myself that I was permitted to come before Your Royal Highness. I came alone, at first, then, foreseeing that I might be detained, either by the will of Your Highness, or by some other impediment, I took my measures. And, at the hour I told you, Milord, at midnight, Miss de Nevers will be brought here and will herself present to Your Highness the pages torn from the Parish Registry by Blanche de Caylus; a precious mandate that she confided to me, fifteen years ago, when, thinking she was giving her child to Philippe de Nevers, she delivered it to me, who, in the moats of Caylus said to her the motto of Nevers, a signal; agreed between her and Duke Philippe.

PRINCESS: It's true, Milord.

REGENT: And the sealed paper is in your power?

LAGARDÈRE: It's in the hands of Miss de Nevers.

GONZAGUE: (to himself) And Miss de Nevers is in mine. (aloud) I dare again address a prayer to Your Highness. I ask you to raise the restraints on Mr. de Lagardère and permit himself; to go under good escort to find himself this terrible evidence that he threatens me with and that I defy him to produce. This monstrous comedy has to be brought to an end, and the act which it must begin rang long ago. See, see, see. (producing his watch and presenting it to Lagardère.)

REGENT: (to Bennivet) Mr. Captain of the Guards, accompany Mr. Lagardère—

PRINCESS: Speak, sir, speak.

GONZAGUE: Yes, sir, speak.

LAGARDÈRE: (who was all the while looking at Gonzague) Ah, Madame! Pray to God I don't arrive too late. (he starts to rush out, but at that moment Cocardasse emerges from the crowd, points his ungloved hand at Lagardère and drops his glove in front of him)

LAGARDÈRE: Ah!

PRINCESS: What's holding you back? Who is preventing you? Why are you going pale?

LAGARDÈRE: Ah, Madame, at the price of my life I would leave the palace. It's a sacred voice that is telling me the daughter of Nevers is in danger.

PRINCESS: My daughter in danger! Oh, I will protect her myself.

LAGARDÈRE: Oh, Madame, at the moment we are speaking she may be dead.

ALL: Dead!

LAGARDÈRE: If she's been kidnapped from me it's to make her disappear. To kill her. Milord, here I am alone, before you, without any proof. But God is just. He will perform a miracle. Three days, Milord, grant me three days. And first let me be free—Milord.

GONZAGUE: Highness, disarm and arrest this man.

REGENT, PRINCESS, & CHAVERNY: Why?

GONZAGUE: Because this man is an assassin!

ALL: An assassin!

GONZAGUE: For fifteen years I've awaited the hour that has finally come. And Philippe de Nevers will be avenged by Philippe d'Orléans.

PRINCESS: Him! Him! Philippe's assassin.

LAGARDÈRE: (to Regent) Milord, I wrote you that in the moats of Caylus I put a mark on the murderer. That mark—there it is, Milord. There it is! (pointing to Gonzague's right hand)

PRINCESS: Oh, my God, my God!

REGENT: Defend yourself, Gonzague, defend yourself.

GONZAGUE: Defend myself! I said that I will accuse, and I do accuse! Yes, Lagardère's sword left a scar, yes, it was in the moats of Caylus that he struck me with the same sword that struck down Philippe de Nevers! Which would have been able to testify against the accomplices of Lagardère, if Lagardère had not slain with his own hand those who could ruin him before you, Milord, before the widow of Nevers, before you, Gentlemen. On my honor, I affirm that this man is the murderer. Consequently, I, Philippe of Mantua, I accuse Henri de Lagardère of murder and rapine, and demand that because of the urgency of the matter it be taken up by the Chambre Ardente.

REGENT: I will do justice to your request, Mr. de Lagardère. You will reply to Mr. de Gonzague—but only before your judges. Deliver your sword to the Captain of my guards.

LAGARDÈRE: (giving his sword) Mr. de Gonzague, if I allow myself to be disarmed, it's because your hour has not come. I will choose my place and my time.

BONNIVET: You are going to follow me, sir.

LAGARDÈRE: (to Regent) Milord, I have a safe conduct from Your Royal Highness. Whatever happens, you wrote it, you signed it.

GONZAGUE: Surprise.

REGENT: It's written, it's signed. This man is free. He has forty-eight hours to cross the frontier.

GONZAGUE: (to Peyrolles) He mustn't escape me this time.

REGENT: You heard me, sir. Leave!

LAGARDÈRE: (tearing up the safe-conduct) Milord, I give you back your word. This freedom you are offering me, which is owed me, I won't take. As for me, in forty-eight hours, with the help of God—that's all I will need to unmask this scoundrel and make my cause triumph. Enough humiliations. I'm raising my head and the honor of my name—on my honor, mine, Henri de Lagardère—who's worth all your honor, I swear that tomorrow, at a like hour, Madame de Nevers will have her daughter, and Nevers his vengeance. Make way for me, gentlemen, I am resuming my right.

(Peyrolles rushes after Lagardère; The Regent supports the Princess.)

CURTAIN

ACT IV
SCENE 9

The corner of the quai of the Tuilleries and the bridge of conferences (today the Ponte-Royal.) A man comes in, worn out by a long run. He stops to support himself on the parapet.

LAGARDÈRE: The cowards! The coward! They were waiting for me at the exit from the Palais; they struck me, and they pursued me to finish me off. Are the wounds I received mortal? Lord, you cannot abandon me again. I have not completed my task. Oh, I hear the step of assassins. And nothing, nothing to fight them with for my life. Ah, this stone. Do I have the strength to raise it? (he picks it up) I'm not mistaken. A single man is coming to me. In the moonlight I can see his naked sword shine. Either he will kill me, or I will have that sword—and then—

COCARDASSE: (enters and looks around—in a low voice.) Hey! Lagardère, Lagardère!

LAGARDÈRE: (raising the stone) I am here.

COCARDASSE: (recoiling) Friend! Praise God! Friend.

LAGARDÈRE: Cocardasse. (lets the stone fall)

COCARDASSE: Ah, there you are, my little Parisian. At last,

I've found you again. I lost you in the midst of this commotion. Hey, why you are shaking, my—

LAGARDÈRE: Quick, quick! A handkerchief to stop this blood that keeps pouring out.

COCARDASSE: Here my little friend. Oh, Hell. What a wound! Who did this to you.

LAGARDÈRE: Peyrolles!

COCARDASSE: Oh, I've got a terrible account to settle with that little rascal. You are shaking.

LAGARDÈRE: (arranging the stone) Leave me where I am.

COCARDASSE: Sit there. Breathe a bit, my little friend. I have straightened out the battlefield for you. When I saw them pursuing you, you that I knew were without arms and wounded, I said to myself, "First, we must rid ourselves of the dogs." I saw you turning left, so I set myself to running to the right, yelling "Lagardère, Lagardère." Then the bloodhounds left the right track to follow mine. And God knows I made them run. When I was out of sight, I retraced my steps by side streets, and here I am.

LAGARDÈRE: Blanche—tell me about Blanche.

COCARDASSE: You understand that when I got to the house at the Rue de Chantre, I no longer found anyone.

LAGARDÈRE: No one?

COCARDASSE: Except my little apprentice who tried to kill me and that I almost demolished. I'll skip that detail. Passepoil escaped my hands only on the condition that he will strangle

Peyrolles, and that he will find the little girl for me again.

LAGARDÈRE: He knows where they took her?

COCARDASSE: He must know by now.

LAGARDÈRE: (rising) Ah, come on, come on.

COCARDASSE: You won't be able to take two steps without fainting like a woman.

LAGARDÈRE: My strength is coming back. I intend to see your apprentice Passepoil, I want him to tell me—

COCARDASSE: Where the child is? As to that, you have nothing to say. Just wait here for Passepoil who should return here to find me. Hey, then, listen, it's not light like that of an elephant. That cannot be his—eh, yes, It's my little Passepoil. Come here, little rascal—and have a look at what Peyrolles has done again.

PASSEPOIL: The little Parisian—wounded.

LAGARDÈRE: Blanche! Where is Blanche?

PASSEPOIL: In a little house belonging to Milord Gonzague in the Rue Saint Magliore.

LAGARDÈRE: You are going to lead me there.

PASSEPOIL: Impossible. All the streets are guarded by henchmen of Gonzague. There are more of them than paving stones.

COCARDASSE (looking) Hush! The jackals have regained the scent.

PASSEPOIL: In that case we are surrounded.

LAGARDÈRE: To put an end to this pursuit these wretches must think me dead. Well, you are going to show them my cadaver.

COCARDASSE: Now that's an idea you've got there. Play dead, my little friend, play dead.

LAGARDÈRE: (stretching out on the ground) You will have finished me.

COCARDASSE: Seeing you pale and bloody as you are they will easily believe it, and won't worry about you any more.

PASSEPOIL: (looking) It's that good Mr. de Peyrolles with a gang of henchmen. Oh, that dear friend who wanted me to kill Lagardère. Me! Son of a whore! I have to get him in my clutches.

PEYROLLES: (enters with his men carrying torches) You've ruined the real track. Come on, come on—Lagardère passed this way, and we no longer have any way of following him except these patches of blood.

COCARDASSE: To find what you are seeking, excellent Mr. de Peyrolles, you have only to go a bit farther.

PEYROLLES: Huh! You are saying?

COCARDASSE: I am saying that Lagardère, only slightly wounded was going to escape you once again. But we were there, my apprentice and I.

PASSEPOIL Yes, We were there.

PEYROLLES: And what did you do?

COCARDASSE (pointing to Lagardère stretched out, motionless.) Look!

PASSEPOIL: Look!

PEYROLLES: (recoiling) Lagardère!

COCARDASSE: Have no fear—he's dead.

PEYROLLES: Are you sure of that?

COCARDASSE & PASSEPOIL: Look!

PEYROLLES: Victory! (to two henchmen) Ruin to the palace and announce very discreetly to Prince de Gonzague, that you have seen Lagardère dead, quite dead this time. (they leave) Ah, we can sleep in peace now. (to the others) My work is done and I am back to the Hotel to rest up a bit. Ouf! Have my chair come and my porters. Go (the henchmen leave)

PASSEPOIL & COCARDASSE: This good Mr. de Peyrolles is satisfied?

PEYROLLES: Yes, yes. It really was possible to kill this Lagardère. I was beginning to think he was invulnerable. And there he is. I had the pleasure of giving him the first blow.

PASSEPOIL: That will be to your account in the next world (aside) and in this one first.

PEYROLLES: I know indeed that this sword blow will come back to me.

PASSEPOIL: No—you don't suspect it.

PEYROLLES: (to himself) First, I will go to the little house in the Rue Saint Magliore. Yes, I've got the key to the garden on me.

LAGARDÈRE (low to Cocardasse) I need that key!

COCARDASSE: (low) You shall have it my little friend. You shall have it.

PEYROLLES: (turning) Hey! It seemed to me that he moved.

PASSEPOIL: It was me letting my hat fall.

PEYROLLES: I would like to know he's a hundred feet underground! (aside) Why, now I think of it, the river's over there. (aloud) Come on the rest of you, let's garrote this demon, gag him, place a stone around his neck and toss him in the water. (to himself) Ah, he won't return from so far away. Huh! What's going on? Ah! (turning he finds himself face to face with Lagardère who's standing bolt upright.)

LAGARDÈRE: (coldly) Garrote this man.

PEYROLLES: Huh! He isn't dead. Help, hel—

COCARDASSE & PASSEPOIL: With pleasure. (they garrote and gag him)

LAGARDÈRE: Put that stone around his neck and toss him in the river.

PASSEPOIL: Very nice! We're doing to the other one what he wanted to do to you.

LAGARDÈRE: Wretched valet. I'll never rest until I've punished your master.

COCARDASSE: (searching Peyrolles) Here's the key to the little house.

PASSEPOIL: Here's a full purse.

COCARDASSE: To you his key—

PASSEPOIL: To us, the rest. And now—

COCARDASSE: (raising Peyrolles with Passepoil's help and balancing him on the parapet.) Now let's execute the justice of Lagardère. (they toss the body into the water.)

LAGARDÈRE: Let's leave.

COCARDASSE: Not on foot. We must take care of you, still, and this good Mr. de Peyrolles has foreseen everything. Here's a chair with porters for you. You will have more bodyguards than His Majesty, Louis XV. First of all, take this cloak (that of Peyrolles) This hat (he puts his hat on him. The porters arrive with a chaise proceeded by a valet carrying a lantern.)

PASSEPOIL: Open quickly. Mr. de Peyrolles is a bit ill. Carry him gently, very gently.

VALET: (with lantern) Where are we going?

LAGARDÈRE: (sticking his head out) Rue Saint Magliore.

COCARDASSE & PASSEPOIL: (acting as porters) Rue Saint Magliore.

CURTAIN

ACT IV
SCENE 10

The Engagement of the Hunchback.

An elegant salon in the little house of Gonzague.

GONZAGUE: Mr. de Peyrolles has not returned yet?

LACROIX: No, Milord, he hasn't reappeared since he brought a truly charming young miss here. A bit sad. (smiling) But one soon becomes gay in our little house.

GONZAGUE: That person is constantly under the guard of Madame Angélique?

LACROIX: Yes, Milord.

GONZAGUE: And the other young girl?

LACROIX: She's remained locked in her room since Mr. de Peyrolles brought her back here. She refuses to open or even respond to Madame Angélique.

GONZAGUE: When Mr. de Peyrolles comes in, tell him to come up right away. If someone comes on his behalf—

LACROIX: I will bring that person. (Lacroix leaves at a sign from Gonzague)

GONZAGUE: (alone) The poor gypsy is weeping over her lost principality, but I will be forced to return it to her—to her misfortune. As for the other young girl so adroitly carried off this evening by Peyrolles there can no longer be any doubt that she is the child of Nevers. I discern Philippe's features in her, and her mother, seeing her won't hesitate for a moment to recognize her as her daughter. But she will not see her. Ah, this Lagardère was a clever man. Before gathering up the inheritance it is necessary to adore her. And she, she'll think only of him, and when she learns that we've finished with this demon, she'll fall struck by a lightning bolt. He was a clever man, that Lagardère,

LACROIX: (announcing) On behalf of Mr. de Peyrolles.

GONZAGUE: At last. (dismissing Lacroix with a gesture; Cocardasse and Passepoil come forward and bow deeply.)

COCARDASSE: (low to Passepoil) Have no fear. We'll speak and speak well.

GONZAGUE: Come here, my braves. Why isn't Peyrolles accompanying you.

COCARDASSE: If he hasn't returned, you mustn't wish ill of this good Mr de Peyrolles.

PASSEPOIL: Oh, no. That wouldn't be fair. It's in no way his fault. I attest to that.

GONZAGUE: You know where he is?

COCARDASSE: More or less.

PASSEPOIL: I suppose he's somewhere between Asnières and Chatou (aside) He must have floated there by now.

GONZAGUE: Why did he leave Paris?

COCARDASSE: No doubt in Milord's service. What is certain is that it wasn't a whim of his own that caused him to make this trip.

PASSEPOIL: No! Oh, no!

GONZAGUE: Since you are here, let Peyrolles go to the devil if he cares to.

PASSEPOL: (aside) Precisely where he's headed.

GONZAGUE: Lagardère is quite dead, right? And it was you who rid me of him.

PASSEPOIL: We were really well behaved in his corner.

GONZAGUE: You will be fittingly paid. What have you done with the cadaver?

PASSEPOIL: That excellent Mr. de Peyrolles himself ordered it thrown in the Seine, and we hurried to obey him.

GONZAGUE: Come! Everything is fine. Miss de Nevers is in my power. Lagardère is dead, and I have in my hands the weapon with which he threatened me. You have faithfully served me, my masters, and you will be rewarded in accordance with your deserts.

COCARDASSE: We have some rightful claims to your gratitude, but Damn it all, we must humbly confess that if we have behaved well in this business, it is thanks to—

GONZAGUE: To Mr. de Peyrolles?

PASSEPOIL and COCARDASEE: No, Milord.

GONZAGUE: You were helped by someone other than Peyrolles?

COCARDASSE: Without this auxiliary, May heaven reward him, Lagardère would have once again slipped through our fingers.

GONZAGUE: And who is this man?

COCARDASSE: I know him only by his hump.

PASSEPOIL: A superb hump.

GONZAGUE: Aesop. It was Aesop.

PASSEPOIL: Oh, his name's Aesop? Pretty name.

COCARDASSE: In short, this disgrace of Nature actually killed Lagardère.

GONZAGUE: What do you mean?

COCARDASSE: Hey, you are going to understand.

PASSEPOIL: (low) Let's say little and say well.

COCARDASSE: (low) Have no fear. (aloud) Here's the thing. At his emergence from the palace Lagardère was surrounded, hemmed in by us then wounded by Mr. de Peyrolles, but wounded slightly. This excellent Mr. de Peyrolles had more zeal than muscle. When we arrived to the rescue, Lagardère was already far away in the little street and alley ways of the Quarter Saint Honoré. We barely recognized his track. We went whichever way chance led us, when a hunchback, hidden behind a pillar that was taller than he was, shouted to us. "He went that way; he's losing blood, he is ours, follow me." And he set out running as if he had nothing on his back. Reaching the quai he pointed out Lagardère to us, who, indeed exhausted by the race and loss of blood, had fallen at the parapet, and it was the hunchback who shouted once more: "Kill him!"

PASEPOIL: Very fine, very fine!

GONZAGUE: Always this hunchback! But why did he do all that?

HUNCHBACK: (appearing) I'm coming to tell you, Milord.

GONZAGUE: Him! Him!

HUNCHBACK: (low) But I will only speak when we are alone.

GONZAGUE: (to Cocardasse) Aesop's share will not diminish yours, my braves. You will soon receive from my treasurer the gift of ten thousand pounds, that I intend to give you.

PASSEPOIL: (aside) Ten thousand pounds.

COCARDASSE: (aside) Eh! Trash! This Prince is just a penny-pincher. Lagardère is worth millions.

(As Gonzague writes his treasurer, The Hunchback signals Cocardasse to come closer.)

HUNCHBACK: You are certain the Parchment is in Gonzague's power?

COCARDASSE: I am sure of it.

HUNCHBACK: Now run to the Hotel Gonzague at all costs. Get to the Princess and deliver my letter to her. Your apprentice will take my letter to Chaverny.

COCARDASSE: All will be accomplished, my little friend.

GONZAGUE: My masters, there are your riches. And country air will agree with you better than that of Paris. Go.

(Cocardasse and Passepoil bow and leave.)

GONZAGUE: Now your turn, Aesop. I know all that you did for me this evening. Speak, what is it you want for your reward?

HUNCHBACK: Milord, what makes you think I came here to claim a salary?

GONZAGUE: All gratuitous service conceals treachery. You will be paid, paid—I insist.

HUNCHBACK: Paid. What makes you think, Milord, that I haven't been paid already? I desired the ruin of Lagardère, and I delivered him to you. I wanted him dead and you killed him.

GONZAGUE: Why did you betray him? Why did you hate him?

HUNCHBACK: Because he was loved.

GONZAGUE: You! Jealous of Lagardère! By some miracle could you be amorous?

HUNCHBACK: That's ridiculous, isn't it? Well, Milord, I am mad, I am in love.

GONZAGUE: (laughing) Hopelessly—

HUNCHBACK: I would be dead if I didn't hope.

GONZAGUE: And who do you love, my poor Aesop?

HUNCHBACK: A woman who loved Lagardère. Now, do you understand my hate for this man? Now do you understand that if I made myself your ally, it was only because I could do nothing against him?

GONZAGUE: Yes, I begin to understand. Up to now, and despite the services you have rendered me, I was wary of you.

HUNCHBACK: And now?

GONZAGUE: Now I believe in your sincerity, since you've told me what led you. Still, you didn't come to me only to make your confession. You have something to ask of me.

HUNCHBACK: It's true.

GONZAGUE: In the end what do you want? Gold to dazzle, to buy what you love?

HUNCHBACK: She cannot be bought.

GONZAGUE: But she will never give herself to you.

HUNCHBACK: You, you can give her to me.

GONZAGUE: Me!

HUNCHBACK: Because you are holding her in your power. I am sure you are seeking a way of ridding yourself of her, and the one I am proposing to you I'm sure you never thought of.

GONZAGUE: What! The object of your monstrous love?

HUNCHBACK: Is Blanche, daughter of Philippe of Lorraine, Duke de Nevers.

GONZAGUE: You know—?

HUNCHBACK: I know the secrets of Lagardère, as I divine your plan. Milord, at all cost, you will cause the legitimate heir to the immense wealth you covet to disappear. You will restore only a pretended daughter of the Duke's whose remaining days to live you are counting in advance. You now have to pass over two cadavers to reach the treasures of Nevers. Well, I will offer you a path and you will avoid the murder of a child. Don't kill Blanche. Give her to me.

GONZAGUE: To you!

HUNCHBACK: To me. I love her not for her title, nor for her gold, but for her youth and her beauty. Give her to me and I will take her far from Paris, from France, from Europe, if you like. Give her to me, not for a mistress but for a wife. She will never use the name of her father but that of her husband.

GONZAGUE: You are in a delirium. She will never agree to it.

HUNCHBACK: That's my concern. Am I not a bit of a sorcerer?

GONZAGUE: (laughing) Yes. If she were blind you would have a chance. But when she sees you—

HUNCHBACK: Let me attempt the project.

GONZAGUE: (gravely) Don't you want to do what Lagardère would have done? Don't you want to take this girl to her mother?

HUNCHBACK: Do you think Aesop would be well received by the proud Princess if he presented himself to her as her son-in-law?

GONZAGUE: You are right. All this would be too comical to be dangerous.

HUNCHBACK: You agree?

GONZAGUE: Blanche will leave this house only to follow her husband. You understand me plainly. Her husband. If she refuses this strange marriage, I am going to propose to her, then you must find some other reward that I can give you. As for this girl—

HUNCHBACK: She will die?

GONZAGUE: She will take these flowers which have only momentarily passed through my hands. She will take this bouquet into her room. She will breathe the intoxicating perfume, and tomorrow, my poor little Aesop, tomorrow, you will be avenged. Save her then, if you can. My friends are coming to sup with me. They will all sign as witnesses the contract drawn up by Master Fidelin, my notary, who I am going to send for.

(he rings; a valet appears) Giraud, I entrust this lad to you.

Lead him to my apartment. Use all your skill in dressing him. Make him seductive. (to Hunchback) When you emerge from my hands, at least you will be presentable. By Jove, I wasn't planning to give a wedding dinner tonight. With you, friend, it's one surprise after another. Let's see, can't you manage something new, still for me?

HUNCHBACK: Perhaps, indeed.

GONZAGUE: Truly. Do you know I wouldn't be surprised if you were the devil in person!

HUNCHBACK: A poor devil, in any event, who can do nothing without you.

GONZAGUE: Giraud's waiting for you! Go, handsome fiancé, and be ready in two hours.

HUNCHBACK: (bowing) In two hours. (he leaves with Giraud)

GONZAGUE: (alone, momentarily) Decidedly, this hunchback is my good angel. He will rid me of Blanche as he delivered me from Lagardère. (noticing Dame Angélique who enters) I was going to have you summoned, Dame Angélique. How's the young lady brought here tonight doing? Better, right?

ANGÉLIQUE: Oh, Milord, I was coming to speak to you about her. Although I no longer fear for her life, I tremble for her reason. It may be necessary to call a doctor.

GONZAGUE: That duty concerns her husband.

DAME ANGÉLIQUE: Her husband?

GONZAGUE: Yes, Dame Angélique. This very night I am

giving this poor child a dowry and a spouse. In a few minutes I myself will go to seek the wedding contract signature for her. Prepare her for this little ceremony, so she'll be ready. (seriously) I wish it. (dismissing Angélique with a gesture at the same moment as guests begin to arrive.) (smiling) Ah, Welcome, Gentlemen.

NAVAILLE: We have news to inform you of. Great news.

GONZAGUE: Let's see.

NAVAILLE: They say Lagardère was caught in a quarrel with Bonnivet's Guards who killed him. Chance has done justice.

GONZAGUE: Better it were the Executioner than Chance. Excuse me, I have an order to give. (he rings and begins writing. A valet appears and he gives him a letter.) This letter goes to Master Fidelin, my notary, immediately. (the valet leaves with the letter.)

Gentlemen, I also have news to apprise you of. Tonight, there's going to be a wedding.

ALL: A wedding!

GONZAGUE: Yes, I'm marrying off one of my protégées.

ALL: Bah!

GONZAGUE: I'm giving her a dowry, and I'm giving her—

NAVAILLE: To whom?

GONZAGUE: To Aesop.

NAVAILLE To the hunchback?

GONZAGUE: We are going to celebrate their engagement.

NAVAILLE: Oh, what a great laugh. Chaverny is really going to laugh.

GONZAGUE: Chaverny?

NAVAILLE: Won't he be one of us?

GONZAGUE: No, I forgot to invite him.

CHAVERNY: (coming in) It was wrong to forget me, my handsome cousin. I would surely have harbored some rancor towards you for that. And if I've come here tonight it's because someone gave me a rendezvous.

GONZAGUE: (laughing) Some lady from the Opera?

CHAVERNY: No—there's nothing funny about the rendezvous, I swear to you. I am not even certain if this letter didn't come from the next world.

GONZAGUE: Could you tell us who gave you the rendezvous at my place?

CHAVERNY: Ah, I'll bet you a thousand to one you cannot guess it?

GONZAGUE: Finally—who is it?

CHAVERNY: Henri, Chevalier de Lagardère.

ALL: But he's dead.

CHAVERNY: I know that perfectly well, but he will succeed in keeping his word. He wrote me that he will be here at two o'clock, and I wager whether it be by door, by window, or by chimney, at two o'clock we will see him arrive.

GONZAGUE: Chaverny takes nothing seriously, not even death.

CHAVERNY: Look at your watches, gentleman. (they all do except Gonzague)

NAVAILLE: Well, it is two o'clock and no one's coming. And no one will come!

CHAVERNY: You are mistaken. I hear steps. They are going to announce Lagardère to you.

(A valet opens the and The Hunchback appears. Everyone breaks out into a burst of laughter. The Hunchback is dressed as an elegant Cavalier with a sword at his side.)

HUNCHBACK: Lagardère! Who's talking about Lagardère here? Who even remembers Lagardère? You, Mr. De Chaverny? You are very good. Aesop, alone will be the guest of the Prince de Gonzague tonight. Aesop alone will be the hero of the festivities. Aesop has almost made himself into a gentleman, see! he wears a sword at his side, a rose in his button-hole; he's getting married; and the fine flower of French nobility is going to witness his marriage contract. All this is quite strange, Mr. De Chaverny. But all this is real. Lagardère is dead. Long live the hunchback who killed him.

CHAVERNY: What, wretch, it was you?

HUNCHBACK I'm the one who's getting married and I am counting on you to be one of my witnesses.

CHAVERNY Oh, that's too much insolence!

GONZAGUE: Aesop is my guest, cousin, and I forbid anyone to insult him. (to Aesop) I am going to find your fiancée. (laughing) Why the devil did you rig yourself out with that sword?

HUNCHBACK: It annoys me a bit, but it completes the outfit.

GONZAGUE: So be it, gentlemen. I am placing Aesop under your protection. You are a man of wit. Make peace with Chaverny. (Gonzague leaves)

HUNCHBACK: Peace is already made, isn't it, Marquis?

NAVAILLE: Ah, no question. Come on, Chaverny, leave this handsome fiancé completely to his luck. Do you actually know who you are going to marry?

HUNCHBACK: I am going to marry the one I love.

CHAVERNY: The one you love? Oh-oh! Aesop is amorous.

NAVAILLE: And of whom, great God?

HUNCHBACK: Of a young girl, beautiful and rich.

NAVAILLE: And unfortunate.

CHAVERNY: And they are giving her to you?

HUNCHBACK: With the dowry of a princess. Yes, Marquis. Ah, I really chose the moment well to put in my request. This young girl was bothering Milord. She annoyed him greatly. And to be rid of her he would have done worse than to give her to me.

CHAVERNY: I think I know the one he intends to sacrifice.

HUNCHBACK: Let's see.

CHAVERNY: That young girl is the one Lagardère was going to present to the Regent—the one he affirmed to be Miss Blanche de Nevers.

HUNCHBACK: Lagardère alone could prove this if he were alive, and Lagardère is dead.

CHAVERNY: Ah, I understand why Lagardère wrote me to come. He was bequeathing me the task of protecting the one he could no longer defend. And by all the Saints, I will do what he would do. Infamous abortion, before your hand can touch that of the orphan, I will break it.

HUNCHBACK: (grasping Chaverny's hand) Wait. By pressing too hard you will ruin the one you wish to serve.

(gaily) Eh, eh! Suppose this young girl accepts without constraint, with joy, even—the hand I am going to extend to her?

CHAVERNY: That's impossible.

HUNCHBACK: If it is, will you break this hand on which the child will be happy to lean for support? It's not yet time to kill me, Marquis, so leave your sword in its scabbard until the hour arrives to test if this blade is good, especially if it is faithful.

CHAVERNY: What do you mean?

HUNCHBACK: Nothing—I remembered myself.

NAVAILLE: Aesop. I announce your fiancée to you. (holding the Hunchback back) Don't reveal yourself too quickly. Let Gonzague prepare the future happiness that awaits you.

BLANCHE: (to Gonzague) Where are you taking me? What do you want from me?

GONZAGUE: My dear child, I repeat to you, you have nothing to fear. You're an orphan, without fortune, without support. A friend has bequeathed you to me, and I intend to offer you a dowry and a spouse.

BLANCHE: My God! Sorrow is driving me mad! I'm not even sure what you are saying to me.

GONZAGUE: I intend to give you a husband, a protector. Won't you consent to see this protector?

BLANCHE: A protector! I had one and they killed him. Yes, they killed him. Because he's not here to protect me.

CHAVERNY: That protector was named Lagardère, right, Miss?

BLANCHE: Yes, yes.

CHAVERNY: In default of Lagardère, absent or dead, I, the Marquis de Chaverny, I declare myself your chevalier. Ah, if violence forced you to enter this house, I swear to God to get you out of it.

GONZAGUE: You forget, too often, that you are in my house, sir. I am offering protection to Miss; I am not imposing it on her.

BLANCHE: Who are you to protect me? I don't know you,

sir. But I feel you are the secret enemy who's pursued me since my childhood. I don't know you, and I am sure you are the one who had me kidnapped; you are the one who had Lagardère killed. I don't want anything from you. Nor from anyone. Nothing except death. Oh, if you truly pity me, kill me, sir, kill me.

(she staggers)

CHAVERNY: (supporting her) She's in a faint. (making her sit down)

GONZAGUE: (to Hunchback) My poor Aesop, your affair is going badly.

HUNCHBACK: It will go better when I manage it myself.

CHAVERNY: (who has made Blanche breathe salts) She's opening her eyes.

HUNCHBACK: (to Gonzague) Then protect me!

GONZAGUE: What are you asking?

HUNCHBACK: I want you to leave me alone with this young girl. In five minutes I shall her triumphed over her resistance.

NAVAILLE: Is this hunchback conceited!

GONZAGUE: Leave you alone with her.

HUNCHBACK: Still distrust? Don't lose sight of me if you like. Just withdraw, leave the doors open. You have an interest in my winning my case. Let me plead it?

GONZAGUE: That's fair.

HUNCHBACK: (low) Do you have a Royal Notary quite ready?

NAVAILLE: He's superb. Word of honor.

GONZAGUE: The notary is there and we will give up our place to you.

NAVAILLE: Let's go. Come, Chaverny.

CHAVERNY: To leave this child—

NAVAILLE: The Hunchback really isn't dangerous. Besides, who's threatening this little one? At her first call won't we be there?

(Navaille pulls Chaverny to the back where the doors remain half open. Blanche has remained unaware of what's going on around her and hasn't noticed the Hunchback slip behind the armchair into which she has fallen.)

HUNCHBACK: (resuming the voice of Lagardère) Blanche!

BLANCHE: (raising her head) Who's calling me?

HUNCHBACK: (hidden behind the chair) Don't you recognize my voice?

BLANCHE: Oh, I'm dreaming. That's his voice and I know he is no more.

HUNCHBACK: Blanche! We are here, on the edge of the abyss. One motion, one gesture and all is lost.

BLANCHE: Henri! Is it you? Is it you?

HUNCHBACK: Silence!

NAVAILLE: (watching) Look at that. He's not clumsy. He's speaking to her before letting her see him.

HUNCHBACK: You are not dreaming, Blanche. Henri is near you. Henri, that they think they've killed, Henri, who under this ridiculous travesty has been able to deceive them and get to you. Gonzague, our enemy, is leaving you free to choose between death and an odious marriage. These men don't believe in Hell. Therefore, obey, Blanche my beloved, obey and by coming to me, not from your heart but from I don't know what bizarre attraction, which for these men will be the work of the demon—fascinated by the hand that enchants you.

BLANCHE: Henri, dear Henri.

NAVAILLE: He's revealing himself bravely to the little one; he's putting himself on his knees before her.

HUNCHBACK: (low) Your hand, let your hand fall into mine. Slowly, very slowly, as if an invisible power forced you to give it to me despite yourself.

(Blanche does what Henri wishes)

CHAVERNY: How she's giving him her hand.

GONZAGUE: The man really is the demon.

HUNCHBACK: Get up now. Fine. Look at me and let your hand fall on my shoulder.

NAVAILLE: He's enchanted her. And in five minutes. Exactly the time he demanded.

HUNCHBACK: Milord, my case is won. Where is the Royal Notary?

CHAVERNY: It's impossible! Miss you did not consent. You cannot consent to belong to this man.

BLANCHE: I was his already, before God!

CHAVERNY: This is sorcery or some infamous snare. What to do?

HUNCHBACK: (low, but in his natural voice) Wait.

CHAVERNY: That voice.

VALET: Master Fidelin.

NAVAILLE: The notary requested.

GONZAGUE: Sir, you've brought a document all prepared?

NOTARY: Milord, I drew it up at your orders. The contract is quite ready, in good and proper form. All that remains is to inscribe the name of the spouses, to get their signatures and those of the witnesses.

GONZAGUE: Place it there, Master Fidelin.

NOTARY: Everything's ready. I'm just waiting for the names of the futures.

GONZAGUE: Your name, friend.

HUNCHBACK: You sign first, Milord. You cannot refuse to be my witness, sign also, gentlemen. For I indeed hope that you will do me this honor. I will write my name myself. Oh, it's a name that will make you laugh. Set the example, Milord.

GONZAGUE: Come on. Pass the pen to me, Master Fidelin. (signs)

ALL: To the married couple! To the married couple!

HUNCHBACK: If we must die here, Blanche, we will die united to each other. Do you want that?

BLANCHE: Yes.

HUNCHBACK: (low to Blanche as he presents the pen to her) Sign Blanche de Nevers. (she signs) My turn now. (he signs)

ALL: It is done.

HUNCHBACK: Yes.

GONZAGUE: You signed with your real name.

(Lagardère stands upright, pulling out his sword and pointing to the signature.)

LAGARDÈRE: Come read this name—come, all.

GONZAGUE: Lagardère!

ALL: Lagardère!

LAGARDÈRE: Lagardère, who never fails to make a rendezvous he gives.

GONZAGUE: (pulling his sword) With death.

ALL: (pulling swords) With death.

LAGARDÈRE (to Chaverny) Everywhere and always. Marquis de Chaverny, you recall?

CHAVERNY: (pulling his sword) Everywhere and always—and against all.

LAGARDÈRE: I knew quite well there would be two of us.

(At that moment Cocardasse and Passepoil arrive, placing themselves, sword in hand beside Chaverny.)

PASSEPOIL: There will be four of us.

COCARDASSE: Who are worth forty—Damn it all!

(As swords are crossed they hear: IN THE NAME OF THE KING!)

(Bonnivet enters followed by his guards.)

BONNIVET: Mr. de Gonzague, Mr. de Lagardère in the name of the King! You are both my prisoners, and both of you are summoned to appear before His Royal Highness The Regent of France, at the request of Blanche de Caylus, widow of Philippe de Lorraine, Duke de Nevers. (swords are lowered) An escort and a post-chaise await you.

GONZAGUE: A post-chaise! Where are you taking us?

BONNIVET I'm forbidden to tell you. (he presents a blindfold)

GONZAGUE: You are going to cover our eyes?

BONNIVET: Order of Milord Regent.

LAGARDÈRE: Mr. De Chaverny, take this child to her mother.

CURTAIN

ACT V
SCENE 11

The moats of Caylus. The same as Scene 2, only torches light the stage. Guards occupy the drawer-bridge, the stairway, the breach at the rear. A table covered with black-velour, some armchairs near the table occupy the right side of the stage.

AT RISE, the Regent, Chaverny, de Villeroy, and other lords are present as well as the Princess and Blanche.

PRINCESS: Relax, dear child, God will protect the brave and generous man who preserved you for my love.

CHAVERNY: This time, Madame, you didn't hesitate to recognize your daughter.

PRINCESS: Oh, no. As soon as you put her in my arms I recognized all of Philippe's features.

REGENT: Pardon me, Madame, for bringing you back to this Château de Caylus which reminds you both of a bloody recollection. It's here that Nevers was murdered in a cowardly way, It's here his murderer, whoever he may be, will be judged and punished. (at a sign from the Regent Gonzague and Lagardère are brought in from different directions. Both are blindfolded. At a sign from the Regent the blindfolds are removed.)

D'ARGENSON. Look, Milord. Mr. de Gonzague is shaking.

REGENT: And Lagardère hasn't changed his expression.

GONZAGUE: The moats of Caylus.

REGENT: Come forward.

GONZAGUE (aside) It's here that Nevers fell, and this time I have my proof.

REGENT: Do the two of you recognize where you are? (they both bow) It's indeed here that Nevers was struck down.

GONZAGUE & LAGARDÈRE: It's here.

GONZAGUE: I thank Your Highness for having chosen this place to put an end to an odious accusation. I presented to my wife, Madame de Gonzague, she whom I affirmed—and she who I still affirm to be the true heir of Philippe. I bring the evidence indicated by the Princess herself. The page torn from the register of the Chapel of Caylus. It is here under triple seal.

REGENT: Madame de Gonzague, do you recognize this piece?

PRINCESS: Yes, I recognize it. Now, speak, Lagardère, speak, my son.

BLANCHE: (kissing her hand) O Mother!

REGENT: Speak, sir.

LAGARDÈRE: Milord, I will deliver all that I promised. I swore on the honor of my name that I would return to Madame de Gonzague the child confided to me at the peril of my life, and I have done it.

PRINCESS: (hugging Blanche.) Yes—yes.

LAGARDÈRE: Milord, I swore to surrender myself to your justice after forty-eight hours of freedom. Before the agreed hour, I gave up my sword. Finally, I swore that I would make my innocence shine forth by unmasking the true culprit, and, with the aid of God, I will keep my oath.

GONZAGUE: Ah, milord, will you suffer any longer that such a wretch accuse me, me—without proof?

LAGARDÈRE: I have my witnesses and I have my proof.

GONZAGUE: (looking around) Witnesses? Where are they?

LAGARDÈRE: There are two. You are the first.

GONZAGUE: This man is mad.

LAGARDÈRE: The second of my witnesses is the tomb.

GONZAGUE: Those who are in the tomb do not speak.

LAGARDÈRE: They will speak when God wishes. Here for witnesses. The dead will speak. As for proof, they are in your hands, My innocence is in the triple-sealed envelope. Refuse to believe it, Providence will strike you with lightning. You yourself produced this parchment, the instrument of your own ruin, and you cannot withdraw it; it belongs to justice and justice hems you in here, on all sides. For to procure this weapon which will strike you, your Peyrolles broke into my dwelling like a thief in the night.

GONZGUE: Milord!

LAGARDÈRE: Go on, are you going to break the seals? There's more in there than a leaf of parchment, the birth certificate of Miss de Nevers.

REGENT: Break the seals, Gonzague.

LAGARDÈRE: No, your hand hesitates and keeps trembling. You've divined there is something else there, right? I am going to tell you what's there. On the back of the parchment, three lines written in blood. Nevers was with me on the night of the murder. It was here, a minute before the battle, he saw the blades of the assassins, and on this leaf, which is in there, with his dagger soaked in his open vein he traced the lines which reveal the crime and the name of the assassin.

REGENT: You are trembling, Gonzague.

GONZAGUE: Me?

LAGARDÈRE: The name is there. The true name in big letters. Break the seal and the dead are going to speak.

(Gonzague recoils before Lagardère and goes close to a torch bearer.)

GONZAGUE: The name is there.

LAGARDÈRE: Read. Let every one know if the name is mine or yours.

(Gonzague with a trembling hand holds the envelope to the flame of the torches.)

PRINCESS: Ah, he's burning the envelope that contains the name of the assassin!

REGENT: (rushing forward) Wretch!

LAGARDÈRE: (pointing to the flaming envelope) The dead have spoken!

REGENT: What was written. Speak fast. You will be believed, because this man has just ruined himself. What was there?

LAGARDÈRE: Nothing, Milord, nothing. Do you hear, Mr. de Gonzague? Your name wasn't there. But you've just written it there yourself.

D'ARGENSON: He has admitted his culpability.

REGENT: Assassin! Assassin!

GONZAGUE: (to Lagardère) You won't enjoy your victory. (he snatches a naked sword held by an officer of the guards and intends to rush Lagardère)

CHAVERNY: (placing himself between them) Yet another murder.

LAGARDÈRE: A sword! A sword!

REGENT: (giving him his) Here. Do justice.

LAGARDÈRE (brandishing his sword) I am here! I am here!

(at the second thrust Gonzague falls.)

COCARDASSE: (hidden behind the guards) Eight!

PASSEPOIL: The count is complete.

LAGARDÈRE: Glory to God! Nevers, I kept my word!

CURTAIN

ABOUT THE AUTHOR

Frank J. Morlock has written and translated many plays since retiring from the legal profession in 1992. His translations have also appeared on Project Gutenberg, the Alexandre Dumas Père web page, Literature in the Age of Napoléon, Infinite Artistries.com, and Munsey's (formerly Blackmask). In 2006 he received an award from the North American Jules Verne Society for his translations of Verne's plays. He lives and works in México.

www.ingramcontent.com/pod-product-compliance
Lightning Source LLC
LaVergne TN
LVHW041623070426
835507LV00008B/414